Descubra Juegos Gratis Online

Disponibles Aquí:

BestActivityBooks.com/FREEGAMES

5 CONSEJOS PARA EMPEZAR

1) CÓMO RESOLVER LAS SOPA DE LETRAS

Los rompecabezas tienen un formato clásico:

- Las palabras se ocultan sin espacios ni guiones,...
- Orientación: Las palabras pueden escribirse hacia delante, hacia atrás, hacia arriba, hacia abajo o en diagonal (pueden estar invertidas).
- Las palabras pueden superponerse o cruzarse.

2) APRENDIZAJE ACTIVO

Junto a cada palabra hay un espacio para anotar la traducción. Para fomentar un aprendizaje activo, un **DICCIONARIO** al final de esta edición te permitirá comprobar y ampliar tus conocimientos. Busca y anota las traducciones, encuéntralas en el puzzle y añádelas a tu vocabulario!

3) MARCAR LAS PALABRAS

Puedes inventar tu propio sistema de marcado. ¿Quizás ya usas uno? También puedes, por ejemplo, marcar las palabras difíciles de encontrar con una cruz, las que te gustan con una estrella, las nuevas con un triángulo, las raras con un diamante, etc.

4) ESTRUCTURAR EL APRENDIZAJE

Esta edición ofrece un **CUADERNO DE NOTAS** muy práctico al final del libro. En vacaciones, de viaje o en casa, podrás organizar fácilmente tus nuevos conocimientos sin necesidad de un segundo cuaderno!

5) ¿HABÉIS TERMINADO TODAS LAS PARRILLAS?

En las últimas páginas de este libro, en la sección **DESAFÍO FINAL**, encontrarás un juego gratis!

¡Rápido y sencillo! Echa un vistazo a nuestra colección de libros de actividades para tu próximo momento de diversión y aprendizaje, ¡a sólo un clic de distancia!

Encuentre su próximo reto en:

BestActivityBooks.com/MiProximoLibro

En sus marcas, listos, ¡Ya!

¿Sabías que hay unas 7.000 lenguas diferentes en el mundo? Las palabras son preciosas.

Nos encantan los idiomas y hemos trabajado duro para crear libros de la más alta calidad para tí. ¿Nuestros ingredientes?

Una selección de temas adecuados para el aprendizaje, tres buenas porciones de entretenimiento, y luego añadimos una cucharada de palabras difíciles y una pizca de palabras raras. Los servimos con cariño y máxima diversión para que puedas resolver los mejores juegos de palabras y te diviertas aprendiendo!

Tu opinión es esencial. Puedes participar activamente en el éxito de este libro dejándonos un comentario. Nos encantaría saber qué es lo que más le ha gustado de esta edición.

Aquí hay un enlace rápido a tu página de pedidos:

BestBooksActivity.com/Opiniones50

Gracias por tu ayuda y diviértete!

Todo el equipo

1 - Ajedrez

```
L  M  P  S  P  O  I  N  T  S  L  M  T  P
B  Z  E  P  A  P  C  L  E  V  E  R  C  O
S  M  B  B  S  P  H  V  B  L  A  C  K  O
A  D  A  W  S  O  A  S  T  F  X  S  W  J
C  U  Y  O  I  N  M  T  R  I  U  Q  E  Q
R  D  S  Z  V  E  P  R  C  U  V  E  J  L
I  I  F  G  E  N  I  A  O  O  L  X  Z  T
F  A  Q  G  G  T  O  T  I  M  E  E  Z  O
I  G  J  U  J  I  N  E  N  C  W  V  S  L
C  O  N  T  E  S  T  G  W  H  I  T  E  E
E  N  E  F  L  E  U  Y  F  K  H  W  U  A
T  A  E  V  Q  I  N  Y  Y  M  I  E  G  R
M  L  C  K  O  G  A  M  E  T  A  N  S  N
Z  I  I  U  D  X  P  L  A  Y  E  R  G  P
```

TO LEARN	BLACK
WHITE	OPPONENT
CHAMPION	PASSIVE
CONTEST	POINTS
DIAGONAL	RULES
STRATEGY	QUEEN
CLEVER	KING
GAME	SACRIFICE
PLAYER	TIME

2 - Agua

```
F L O O D C D A Q T A C O T
I R R I G A T I O N W A C Q
T A Y W G R D F J B Q N E L
E V A P O R A T I O N A A A
G E Y S E R M M H J A L N K
H M E Q V D P S H O W E R E
U X C G X D R I N K A B L E
R S T E A M R U V E V I T K
R L L O L G A D X E E V Z T
I H U M I D I T Y J S C W W
C W K C P C N K S R I V E R
A F R O S T E W N Y T D S P
N U Y P O N W M O N S O O N
E K M H X N K N W T E J B F
```

CANAL	LAKE
SHOWER	RAIN
EVAPORATION	MONSOON
GEYSER	SNOW
FROST	OCEAN
ICE	WAVES
HUMIDITY	DRINKABLE
HURRICANE	IRRIGATION
DAMP	RIVER
FLOOD	STEAM

3 - Granja #2

```
B Y F I A D L J S U K O I I
E J V Y I C H Z H W K Q E R
E C E V O M Q K E H R Y B R
H M G M N Z W Q P B Y S R I
I I E T F H E W H G A F X G
V I T U C O R N E S C R A A
E Z A E V L O Y R I E U N T
E Y B F J L B D D V Z I I I
M I L K F A R M E R Z T M O
M L E S W M E A D O W Z A N
S O R C H A R D U C K K L L
Q G X S E B A R L E Y S A
D V Y D A S E R T I J U B M
T R A C T O R P C X Q E V B
```

FARMER	LLAMA
ANIMALS	CORN
BARLEY	SHEEP
BEEHIVE	SHEPHERD
FOOD	DUCK
LAMB	MEADOW
FRUIT	IRRIGATION
BARN	TRACTOR
ORCHARD	WHEAT
MILK	VEGETABLE

4 - Mueble

```
B  A  Z  C  G  K  D  E  S  K  M  O  I  M
E  R  D  H  U  B  O  O  K  C  A  S  E  A
N  M  R  A  J  R  P  I  L  L  O  W  K  T
C  O  E  I  B  O  T  I  G  K  P  F  T
H  I  S  R  Y  I  E  A  P  S  L  M  A  R
F  R  S  J  C  A  R  M  I  R  R  O  R  E
C  E  E  Y  S  F  U  T  O  N  M  A  B  S
S  U  R  W  B  D  G  J  B  W  S  R  E  S
I  H  S  L  A  M  P  M  V  R  I  M  D  C
N  I  E  H  H  A  M  M  O  C  K  C  V  O
S  W  H  L  I  G  C  X  E  D  Q  H  Y  U
X  Z  K  U  V  O  B  J  J  Z  W  A  G  C
L  O  W  Y  Y  E  N  Q  I  M  L  I  G  H
R  Q  K  S  N  R  S  S  N  N  I  R  V  X
```

RUG
PILLOW
ARMOIRE
BENCH
BED
CUSHIONS
MATTRESS
CURTAINS
DRESSER
DESK

MIRROR
BOOKCASE
SHELVES
FUTON
HAMMOCK
LAMP
CHAIR
ARMCHAIR
COUCH

5 - Pesca

```
C J B E W M O O H Q K O B W
G N K N E W N C D Q H S O S
I E U Q I S E E Z Y W B A K
L X B J G H B A I T A E T B
L A G B H P O N S G T A Z G
S G K S T K O O T J E C V V
P G W E C O O K K X R H E H
A E I A L L N C B A S K E T
T R R S X A D K E Q J P D
I A E O L F K R J L S H I L
E T X N J E Q U I P M E N T
N I O N A F I N S V D Z T O
C O I F W A O R E D E F M N
E N H Z W N E G F Y J R C T
```

WATER	HOOK
FINS	LAKE
BOAT	JAW
GILLS	OCEAN
WIRE	PATIENCE
BAIT	WEIGHT
BASKET	BEACH
COOK	RIVER
EQUIPMENT	SEASON
EXAGGERATION	

6 - Aviones

```
M  B  P  A  I  R  A  H  S  X  I  L  G  C
O  Z  A  T  H  L  L  V  E  E  I  M  N  O
W  B  S  M  Y  Q  T  A  Y  I  U  L  T  N
M  A  S  O  D  Z  I  L  N  K  G  K  E  S
D  L  E  S  R  Q  T  A  S  D  H  H  I  T
I  L  N  P  O  F  U  E  L  S  I  C  T  R
R  O  G  H  G  O  D  B  P  K  S  N  P  U
E  O  E  E  Z  E  J  Y  Y  T  E  G  C  C
C  N  R  R  N  P  I  L  O  T  O  N  D  T
T  T  L  E  A  C  R  E  W  V  R  G  E  I
I  A  D  V  E  N  T  U  R  E  Y  I  S  O
O  P  R  O  P  E  L  L  E  R  S  N  I  N
N  T  U  R  B  U  L  E  N  C  E  E  G  V
B  C  W  A  C  Y  S  R  X  G  Q  A  N  I
```

AIR	DESIGN
ALTITUDE	BALLOON
HEIGHT	PROPELLERS
LANDING	HYDROGEN
ATMOSPHERE	HISTORY
ADVENTURE	ENGINE
SKY	PASSENGER
FUEL	PILOT
CONSTRUCTION	CREW
DIRECTION	TURBULENCE

7 - Tipos de Cabello

```
S U C R S C S W C D Q U K O
I S U N H J H E A L T H Y W
L G R Z I Q O I W V H G Y F
V Z L U N M R A X G Y Z K J
E Y Y A Y J T B W G K V J N
R Y L C E I H R W B L O N D
L S W E B X U A H U C E O K
B R A I D E D I I T T P P B
L S Y V T A J D T H H Q D L
K N N W T R B S E I I E G A
C U R L S Q A R P N C U D C
S D W C O K L M O B K F U K
K J E T F N D O O W Q G F I
H N P N T X G R A Y N D R Y
```

WHITE	WAVY
SHINY	SILVER
BALD	CURLY
SHORT	CURLS
THIN	BLOND
GRAY	HEALTHY
THICK	DRY
LONG	SOFT
BROWN	BRAIDED
BLACK	BRAIDS

8 - Ciencia Ficción

```
W V R O B O T S F U E I T M
U O P E C U T O P I A C E Y
X E R G A L A X Y F R S C S
U X E L U L Z W D D G E H T
A P S D D V I B O O K S N E
H L B I N D M S F B G P O R
E O D I S T A N T D U L L I
X S P L A A G A X I H A O O
T I Q L T K I R Y V C N G U
R O V U O E N K J A I E Y S
E N M S M A A V R E N T M Q
M E O I I O R A C L E S E P
E B X O C N Y K I M M A Y U
Q F A N T A S T I C A T W H
```

ATOMIC	BOOKS
CINEMA	MYSTERIOUS
DISTANT	WORLD
EXPLOSION	ORACLE
EXTREME	PLANET
FANTASTIC	REALISTIC
FIRE	ROBOTS
GALAXY	TECHNOLOGY
ILLUSION	UTOPIA
IMAGINARY	

9 - Juguetes

```
R  B  A  L  L  K  P  C  V  B  G  C  I  C
T  O  T  B  O  C  U  A  Q  P  O  R  D  H
R  O  B  S  G  T  Z  R  I  R  B  A  O  E
U  K  R  O  W  W  Z  N  B  N  L  F  T  S
C  S  P  Y  T  C  L  A  Y  H  T  T  R  S
K  A  Q  T  Y  J  E  I  H  Z  W  S  A  F
K  I  T  E  Y  Z  E  D  R  U  M  S  I  A
C  R  R  F  Q  S  M  I  A  M  O  J  N  V
J  P  B  I  C  Y  C  L  E  R  W  H  C  O
X  L  I  M  A  G  I  N  A  T  I  O  N  R
I  A  I  T  Q  H  X  G  A  M  E  S  C  I
U  N  H  Z  Y  W  T  P  W  D  O  L  L  T
B  E  O  Q  J  R  J  B  M  O  M  U  D  E
Q  L  L  O  Y  X  K  D  C  P  B  Y  X  G
```

CHESS
CLAY
CRAFTS
AIRPLANE
BOAT
BICYCLE
BALL
TRUCK
CAR
KITE

FAVORITE
IMAGINATION
GAMES
BOOKS
DOLL
PAINTS
ROBOT
PUZZLE
DRUMS
TRAIN

10 - Circo

```
H X J Q M U K V L L A F X A
M A G I C A R C C F I I Z N
T J H J U C G K G F W O K I
E N T E R T A I N K E K N M
B Z A A U F F M C A N D Y A
S P E C T A T O R I Q D Z L
C J L R B I R N B U A Q V S
L U E O A Z G K P M D N Q Q
O G P B L D C E P A R A D E
W G H A L J O Y R M U S I C
N L A T O T E N T Z S H M K
R E N G O T R I C K S O J Z
L R T K N O I K A Y E W D A
V H A T S D C O S T U M E X
```

ACROBAT	MAGIC
ANIMALS	MAGICIAN
CANDY	JUGGLER
TENT	MONKEY
PARADE	SHOW
ELEPHANT	MUSIC
ENTERTAIN	CLOWN
SPECTATOR	TIGER
BALLOONS	COSTUME
LION	TRICK

11 - Rellenar

```
B A S K E T T U B E R T H D
A U D M F U B R B A G O Y U
S R C G E B A C A R T O N K
I N G K C O R Q Y Y B X K G
N H K R E X R D R A W E R A
D Q E N Q T E P B U S K D C
E Q A V F O L D E R U R L N
V N J A R E M N H O I R U A
B H V S B D H A S M T M E C
K L B E Q W M R P O C K E T
U J J K L R B Z U V A U M C
X H C Y B O T T L E S V U J
O M P J T Y P A C K E T A O
R L W D M I A E C W A H D A
```

TRAY
TUB
BARREL
BAG
POCKET
BOTTLE
BOX
DRAWER
FOLDER
CARTON

BASKET
BUCKET
BASIN
VASE
SUITCASE
PACKET
ENVELOPE
JAR
TUBE

12 - Granja #1

```
C A L F E N C E D P V G S A
P W S A G R I C U L T U R E
Z J E H R X F D O G O A T M
G U E G I H L O M W C R O W
L M D E C S W N H O N E Y I
F A S P E F A K O Y Z M Y S
N N N V L V T E R G C X V C
B E E D N Y E Y S B B A G O
F V C Q S F R K E V A M T T
N F D C H I C K E N C I Z L
G N E S W E O O A I P T R M
O E I N J L H A Y V V V O W
F Y R E C D F Q Y E X R P D
F E R T I L I Z E R Y W Q X
```

BEE	CAT
AGRICULTURE	HAY
WATER	HONEY
RICE	DOG
DONKEY	CHICKEN
HORSE	SEEDS
GOAT	CALF
FIELD	LAND
CROW	COW
FERTILIZER	FENCE

13 - Camping

```
H A T F U U L V M S M T A K
F U L P I C A N O E B H D V
O H N G M R K E R C E I V L
R N A T U R E R M O O N E A
E X K R I T K W E M P S N N
S I F E H N G B Q P J E T T
T V O F N P G V U A C C U E
T O V P C J U V I S A T R R
X C V Q R J G P P S B S E N
M O U N T A I N M V I G S F
T R E E S R U S E P N W Y B
E M E E Z L V Z N W F U T M
H A M M O C K X T O P G L A
Q K I Y E U A N I M A L S P
```

ANIMALS	FIRE
ADVENTURE	HAMMOCK
TREES	INSECT
FOREST	LAKE
COMPASS	LANTERN
CABIN	MOON
CANOE	MAP
HUNTING	MOUNTAIN
ROPE	NATURE
EQUIPMENT	HAT

14 - Fruta

```
N A P R I C O T L A W D X T
Q E I R A S P B E R R Y J B
I C C H I S F J M M G A U G
L X H T S Z T O X I M W D
R T E G A Z D O N I F D E D
E R R P R O R A N G E A O
K Q R A P P I N E A P P L E
M K Y P L Y P N P P E A C H
E A I E E G G X E D S P O K
L P C W L G U A V A M A C D
O E H M I L M D W L E Y O W
N A V O C A D O B A N A N A
K R M A N G O F L F W S U N
C B G Y R X Z B E R R Y T U
```

AVOCADO
APRICOT
BERRY
CHERRY
COCONUT
RASPBERRY
GUAVA
KIWI
LEMON
MANGO

APPLE
PEACH
MELON
ORANGE
NECTARINE
PAPAYA
PEAR
PINEAPPLE
BANANA
GRAPE

15 - Geología

```
S  M  D  F  H  I  L  O  W  N  C  B  C  G
L  A  U  M  O  P  D  B  G  L  A  Q  R  W
A  Y  L  K  R  S  L  F  X  A  V  V  Y  S
I  U  F  T  N  T  S  A  X  V  E  R  S  T
S  T  O  N  E  A  S  I  T  A  R  G  T  A
A  C  I  D  R  L  M  R  L  E  N  M  A  L
C  O  R  A  L  A  E  G  Y  P  A  Q  L  A
G  H  C  A  L  C  I  U  M  C  K  U  S  G
X  T  C  O  N  T  I  N  E  N  T  A  J  M
P  D  W  N  L  I  G  E  Y  S  E  R  W  I
L  A  Y  E  R  T  M  N  Q  C  G  T  O  T
S  R  M  I  N  E  R  A  L  S  A  Z  M  E
E  A  R  T  H  Q  U  A  K  E  Y  R  S  S
E  R  O  S  I  O  N  V  O  L  C  A  N  O
```

ACID	STALAGMITES
CALCIUM	FOSSIL
LAYER	GEYSER
CAVERN	LAVA
CONTINENT	PLATEAU
CORAL	MINERALS
CRYSTALS	STONE
QUARTZ	SALT
EROSION	EARTHQUAKE
STALACTITE	VOLCANO

16 - Plantas

```
B E A N F W F K A T B G H C
C A C T U S U J G B E R R Y
R Z M V F L O R A P F A Z Q
Z O S B L I R X R C O S F L
L S O B O J V U D T L S E E
H D Q T W O E Y E B I M R A
Q P Z J E W K G N P A T T F
G E D Q R B U A Y B G W I A
K T T R E E S L D O E U L L
X A X K B J L R T T H H I T
U L F O R E S T V A J E Z X
H N C F D M O S S N L J E B
B U S H H W Z D G Y F U R Z
V E G E T A T I O N E X K S
```

BUSH	FOLIAGE
TREE	BEAN
BAMBOO	IVY
BERRY	GRASS
FOREST	LEAF
BOTANY	GARDEN
CACTUS	MOSS
FERTILIZER	PETAL
FLOWER	ROOT
FLORA	VEGETATION

17 - Suministros de Arte

```
C A M E R A G G M C I I A M
H R P E N C I L S L N D C O
A C E W X M E U Z A K B R Q
I O B A L D M E E Y N Q Y O
R L R T T H U F P A F A L L
F O U E A I J N A L S K I W
N R S R B E V C I I J E C W
S S H C L E P I N O I L L A
M I E O E G P A T Y X O W T
L D S L E G A B S Y Q F M E
Z E K O I E P S H T X U U R
V A P R I B E R A S E R B N
R S P S O V R S K S P L T S
M W D T C U M P H Z E U S I
```

OIL
ACRYLIC
WATERCOLORS
WATER
CLAY
ERASER
EASEL
CAMERA
BRUSHES
COLORS

CREATIVITY
IDEAS
PENCILS
TABLE
PAPER
PASTELS
GLUE
PAINTS
CHAIR
INK

18 - Jardín

```
H U I R N N Q F R B N Z H O
T R A M P O L I N E H E O R
L A X A O F W X G R A S S C
N K J U N B E N C H M U E H
R E A P D Y E N N I M U N A
P S O I L M D E C E O P Q R
P O T H B F S A S E C T Y D
G A R A G E F S F B K J W H
C I E C B U S H G A R D E N
C W E U H Z F O F L O W E R
V H M P A S R V C G R Y S L
O V H U H Y T E R R A C E A
V G K T C Y N L M K X S T W
I I D B Q J M O J J C B C N
```

BUSH   GARDEN
TREE   WEEDS
BENCH   HOSE
LAWN   SHOVEL
POND   PORCH
FLOWER   RAKE
GARAGE   SOIL
HAMMOCK   TERRACE
GRASS   TRAMPOLINE
ORCHARD   FENCE

19 - Países #2

```
A I N Q H Y D J A M A I C A
U N M Y D P E U G A N D A R
S D R H B U N H S L T U F M
T O A U O Q M S U O R K A Q
R N L A O S A K U X Z R U W
A E B F G W R B D D J A S R
L S A R T R K S W A A I T U
I I N A K S E M Y X R N R S
A A I N C C O E E R Y E I S
R X A C I O N W C F I J A I
W X M E X I C O R E P A T A
P A K I S T A N V A O P V I
I P G U I R E L A N D A Y Y
E T H I O P I A L Z Y N J C
```

ALBANIA	JAPAN
AUSTRALIA	LAOS
AUSTRIA	MEXICO
DENMARK	PAKISTAN
ETHIOPIA	RUSSIA
FRANCE	SYRIA
GREECE	SUDAN
INDONESIA	UKRAINE
IRELAND	UGANDA
JAMAICA	

20 - Tecnología

```
E  N  V  J  I  F  Z  V  F  C  C  L  X  C
S  O  F  T  W  A  R  E  I  Z  Z  V  V  U
W  V  L  B  K  G  N  B  J  R  S  I  A  R
C  F  I  L  E  F  C  R  V  Q  T  R  J  S
O  S  N  O  B  N  D  Z  H  D  B  U  Y  O
M  G  T  G  B  R  O  W  S  E  R  S  A  R
P  C  E  A  Y  V  D  V  U  K  D  E  M  L
U  S  R  F  T  X  X  A  Q  X  I  C  E  Z
T  U  N  O  E  I  E  S  T  Y  G  U  S  W
E  G  E  N  S  K  S  J  Y  A  I  R  S  G
R  U  T  T  E  T  C  T  I  R  T  I  A  S
S  C  R  E  E  N  J  Z  I  B  A  T  G  X
C  A  M  E  R  A  Z  Q  C  C  L  Y  E  F
R  E  S  E  A  R  C  H  N  O  S  Q  V  B
```

FILE
BLOG
BYTES
CAMERA
CURSOR
DATA
DIGITAL
STATISTICS
FONT
INTERNET

RESEARCH
MESSAGE
BROWSER
COMPUTER
SCREEN
SECURITY
SOFTWARE
VIRTUAL
VIRUS

21 - Números

```
T Z L L I V B A G S E D I E
D E C I M A L X S B I K A I
E R N I N E T E E N G M E G
V O G V K Z N Z V E H E F H
B F S I X N X I E W T B O T
D I I V Y L Y Z N C W X U E
T V X F F O U R T E E N R E
W E T A T U H M W Y L B H N
E L E V H E L Q O O V I K X
N F E K R Y E K B P E A X Z
T Y N S E V E N T E E N G X
Y W V A E M O T G D V Z H N
H C D Y R D F Z C O V Z J X
T H I R T E E N R Q A C U B
```

FOURTEEN	TWELVE
ZERO	TWO
FIVE	NINE
FOUR	EIGHT
DECIMAL	FIFTEEN
NINETEEN	SIX
EIGHTEEN	SEVEN
SIXTEEN	THIRTEEN
SEVENTEEN	THREE
TEN	TWENTY

22 - Mitología

```
R T C Y C U L T U R E R A P
Q D A G T Z I H D N K M I B
H E A V E N G U K D Z U R E
W I O H X G H N X C Q U A L
R X P K D X T D G X F E G I
A L Z J Q K N E L H E R O E
V B Y W C C I R A E L C C F
M O R T A L N J B W G R M S
I R K O F P G N Y A Q E O M
B E H A V I O R R R Z A N F
C R E A T I O N I R B T S D
D I S A S T E R N I X U T W
S T R E N G T H T O B R E L
J E A L O U S Y H R R E R A
```

JEALOUSY	WARRIOR
HEAVEN	HERO
BEHAVIOR	LABYRINTH
CREATION	LEGEND
BELIEFS	MONSTER
CREATURE	MORTAL
CULTURE	LIGHTNING
DISASTER	THUNDER
STRENGTH	

23 - Ecología

```
L T S D D I V E R S I T Y V
G L O B A L S M E M V M P E
Y T K U N I F A U N A K W G
T I K S U S T A I N A B L E
R E S O U R C E S K F N H T
N R P U N T H A B I T A T A
A X E D R O U G H T B T C T
T C C M B V D D R U E U D I
U L I A A A I E A H J R V O
R I E R G R F V X I Z E Y N
A M S S J I U A D R D S Z
L A Z H X E Q N F L O R A B
R T F E X T L Y E H D S A K
G E L W G Y C P L A N T S V
```

CLIMATE
DIVERSITY
SPECIES
FAUNA
FLORA
GLOBAL
HABITAT
MARINE
NATURAL

NATURE
MARSH
PLANTS
RESOURCES
DROUGHT
SUSTAINABLE
SURVIVAL
VARIETY
VEGETATION

24 - Herramientas

```
E  O  M  A  O  H  B  R  M  M  H  W  S  L
O  F  H  F  O  N  Y  A  U  A  X  E  T  A
C  A  B  L  E  N  N  B  B  L  J  K  A  D
R  C  I  W  U  V  A  I  K  L  E  N  P  D
W  Y  N  R  Y  S  H  O  V  E  L  R  L  E
A  Z  L  E  M  C  B  H  W  T  I  O  E  R
N  Q  L  D  J  I  O  S  Q  H  O  B  R  Z
Q  M  S  H  E  S  T  A  P  L  E  W  Z  K
G  L  T  Q  V  S  O  A  L  X  N  E  G  N
H  L  R  A  Z  O  R  S  C  R  E  W  L  I
R  K  U  C  T  R  C  A  E  K  Q  T  T  F
P  L  I  E  R  S  H  A  M  M  E  R  I  E
C  B  Z  S  T  O  X  Y  P  M  J  V  I  K
Q  I  F  Q  R  O  P  E  J  O  G  M  G  H
```

PLIERS	HAMMER
TORCH	MALLET
CABLE	RAZOR
KNIFE	SHOVEL
ROPE	GLUE
LADDER	RULER
STAPLE	WHEEL
STAPLER	SCISSORS
AXE	SCREW

25 - Casa

```
K F Q H W G L I B R A R Y A
X E E I F L O O R G R H W T
C N U S I Z H Q O A R A A T
K C G C R B D O O R U H L I
Q E A G E O E V M D G Q L C
P U R K P S O D A E L A M P
J Y A I L Y H F R N I V G Q
Z D G T A N G O F O G I Y M
K J E C C D E Q W M O F R I
H Z H H E F A U C E T M B R
B A S E M E N T A Q R I Q R
C W I N D O W D X R H D X O
G S K J O Y G P V M N R V R
I M Z K C T P S Z T Q A N X
```

RUG
ATTIC
LIBRARY
FIREPLACE
KITCHEN
BEDROOM
SHOWER
BROOM
MIRROR
GARAGE

FAUCET
GARDEN
LAMP
WALL
FLOOR
DOOR
BASEMENT
ROOF
FENCE
WINDOW

26 - Artes Visuales

```
M A S T E R P I E C E C C P
D A V A R N I S H J A O E A
Y L R P C H A L K B S M R I
F P L E X T D S J T E P A N
P E N N P D F P N E L O M T
S R S C Z O A O W K I S I I
C S T I D N R C L A Y I C N
U P E L G G T N O X T S G
L E N Z Q P I Z R K F I L M
P C C J V H S I F A D O P C
T T I U S K T W Y K I N O U
U I L C R E A T I V I T Y W
R V P H O T O G R A P H R T
E E A R C H I T E C T U R E
```

CLAY	PHOTOGRAPH
ARCHITECTURE	PENCIL
ARTIST	MASTERPIECE
VARNISH	FILM
EASEL	PERSPECTIVE
WAX	PAINTING
CERAMICS	STENCIL
COMPOSITION	PEN
CREATIVITY	PORTRAIT
SCULPTURE	CHALK

27 - Escuela #2

```
W P E N C I L C E S A G C F
J B A C K P A C K H S R O L
F U E P G A M E S N C A M Z
Q S J T E A C H E R I M P C
Z G G J Y R H G J V E M U L
E D U C A T I O N J N A T O
L I T E R A T U R E C R E T
A C A D E M I C U H E X R H
D I C T I O N A R Y O T Q E
S U P P L I E S N B O O K S
V O I X K R E A D I N G H J
C A L E N D A R T Z G Q J I
M S C I S S O R S C K P D T
W R N Y T C L I B R A R Y T
```

ACADEMIC	READING
BUS	BOOKS
LIBRARY	LITERATURE
CALENDAR	BACKPACK
SCIENCE	COMPUTER
DICTIONARY	PAPER
EDUCATION	TEACHER
GRAMMAR	CLOTHES
GAMES	SUPPLIES
PENCIL	SCISSORS

28 - Selva Tropical

```
M  E  P  I  V  O  W  A  S  H  I  R  P  I
G  A  Z  A  X  O  W  M  U  Y  N  E  R  N
M  D  M  M  O  S  S  P  R  D  D  S  E  S
R  I  H  M  J  Q  S  H  V  C  I  T  S  E
E  N  W  H  A  B  Y  I  I  O  G  O  E  C
S  J  U  N  G  L  E  B  V  M  E  R  R  T
P  P  Q  T  A  S  S  I  A  M  N  A  V  S
E  P  E  W  W  J  L  A  L  U  O  T  A  V
C  A  D  C  D  K  S  N  R  N  U  I  T  T
T  N  I  B  I  R  D  S  A  I  S  O  I  V
U  V  D  I  V  E  R  S  I  T  Y  N  O  G
R  E  F  U  G  E  S  A  T  Y  U  M  N  A
G  B  O  T  A  N  I  C  A  L  H  R  O  L
C  L  O  U  D  S  C  L  I  M  A  T  E  Z
```

AMPHIBIANS	NATURE
BOTANICAL	CLOUDS
CLIMATE	BIRDS
COMMUNITY	PRESERVATION
DIVERSITY	REFUGE
SPECIES	RESPECT
INDIGENOUS	RESTORATION
INSECTS	JUNGLE
MAMMALS	SURVIVAL
MOSS	

29 - Colores

```
I Y O S W W E W S U O E R E
R N Y E L L O W V D R E D L
C M D P I N K D S U A B C M
G B E I G E E E X W N L T P
B S V A G G R E E N G A C U
R I Q Z T O I K Y W E C Y R
T F F U C H S I A B H K A P
K U B R X R H V E L G I N L
M J Z E W M I T T U U M T E
M A G E N T A M U E H G J E
B R O W N Z P H S L Z W H L
V I O L E T B W B O L G Y Y
Y J C L N L G R E Y N F I T
W G Q M N P M P H F Y B K B
```

YELLOW	MAGENTA
BLUE	BROWN
AZURE	ORANGE
BEIGE	BLACK
WHITE	PURPLE
CRIMSON	RED
CYAN	PINK
FUCHSIA	SEPIA
GREY	GREEN
INDIGO	VIOLET

30 - Adjetivos #1

```
H U A O L Y M M S W K A G B
E A M O A R O M A T I C E R
A O B O R M T U R T J T N I
V A I N G P O X N F V I E G
Y B T B E E R D R G K V R H
H S I D A R K T E E M E O T
K O O V Z F K S E R I O U S
H L U C M E C Q E D N V S U
K U S L F C I N N O C E N T
G T G J P T S L O W R R K Q
I E B E A T T R A C T I V E
I M P O R T A N T H T X E V
H O N E S T V A L U A B L E
V H S I S J S B F Q V U K Q
```

ABSOLUTE	IMPORTANT
ACTIVE	INNOCENT
AMBITIOUS	YOUNG
AROMATIC	SLOW
ATTRACTIVE	MODERN
BRIGHT	DARK
HUGE	PERFECT
GENEROUS	HEAVY
LARGE	SERIOUS
HONEST	VALUABLE

31 - Familia

```
G G R A N D F A T H E R D H
B R O T H E R A O R I A A U
M T A N C E S T O R Y I U S
G O Z N N I E C E Y B J G B
S G T R D S I S T E R T H A
K C S H B S X X M Q C L T N
L C H N E R O W F L O I E D
Y O M I E R N N W I F E R F
A U N T L M A T E R N A L Z
U S G J D D E A H T P Y N C
N I K J E C H I L D R E N H
C N E P H E W O Y Y N X I I
L Z G R A N D M O T H E R L
E F A T H E R P J D J R D D
```

GRANDMOTHER
GRANDFATHER
ANCESTOR
WIFE
SISTER
BROTHER
DAUGHTER
CHILDHOOD
MOTHER
HUSBAND

MATERNAL
GRANDSON
CHILD
CHILDREN
FATHER
COUSIN
NIECE
NEPHEW
AUNT
UNCLE

32 - Disciplinas Científicas

```
M N S M I N E R A L O G Y U
E E O A R C H A E O L O G Y
C U C L I N G U I S T I C S
H R I C H E M I S T R Y C E
A O O I Z V A B O T A N Y C
N L L I M M U N O L O G Y O
I O O Q Q T G I A P F D Q L
C G G R I P I E I T F W N O
S Y Y I H B B I O L O G Y G
N U T R I T I O N L W M U Y
W A L P S Y C H O L O G Y X
P H Y S I O L O G Y G G W F
B I O C H E M I S T R Y Y M
P A S T R O N O M Y O H Y L
```

ANATOMY	IMMUNOLOGY
ARCHAEOLOGY	LINGUISTICS
ASTRONOMY	MECHANICS
BIOLOGY	MINERALOGY
BIOCHEMISTRY	NEUROLOGY
BOTANY	NUTRITION
ECOLOGY	PSYCHOLOGY
PHYSIOLOGY	CHEMISTRY
GEOLOGY	SOCIOLOGY

33 - Gatos

```
Q R H X E F T Y P N P R Z M
L E K U O L A G A C A P P O
C N R L N I I Q T R W G P U
F U N N Y T L W H A N C J S
G C Q S L T E K T Z D A R E
C L A W H L K R Z Y F H F C
Q G I D Z E H I V Q A U Y W
M X M Q C U R I O U S B R I
I N D E P E N D E N T Z L L
S L E E P N M V Y H A F I D
A F F E C T I O N A T E Z M
P E R S O N A L I T Y S H Y
P L A Y F U L B V D K R X S
F L X M E F E B L Q U F R O
```

AFFECTIONATE	CRAZY
HUNTER	PAW
TAIL	PERSONALITY
CURIOUS	FUR
SLEEP	LITTLE
CLAW	MOUSE
FUNNY	FAST
YARN	WILD
INDEPENDENT	SHY
PLAYFUL	

34 - Cocina

```
R E F R I G E R A T O R I H
P N A P K I N F O R K S I U
C U P S D K E F D T E L U X
H P D P C H N U C J T C N L
O M T O E A T I Q F T J E W
P I O O F O O D V R L U Q P
S R J N J R C P U E E G D O
T K A S U D E Y F C S A I L
I S S P O N G E X I D N D E
C F K I A T E M Z P B I G L
K G K C G R I L L E V O V A
S M D E A P R O N Y R V W D
M J O S O M C P V B B E F L
U N Z M C B Y Z I U M N G E
```

KETTLE	OVEN
TO EAT	JUG
FOOD	CHOPSTICKS
FREEZER	GRILL
SPOONS	RECIPE
LADLE	REFRIGERATOR
KNIVES	NAPKIN
APRON	CUPS
SPICES	BOWL
SPONGE	FORKS

35 - Escuela #1

```
D  I  V  M  J  N  W  H  I  P  Y  T  H  A
E  D  O  A  P  U  C  I  L  L  T  U  C  N
L  X  B  T  E  M  A  R  K  E  R  S  R  S
O  U  A  H  P  B  L  I  B  R  A  R  Y  W
B  V  N  M  D  E  S  K  X  W  L  B  C  E
U  V  C  C  S  R  N  I  G  K  P  O  U  R
Y  S  M  K  H  S  F  C  J  D  H  O  T  S
T  O  L  E  A  R  N  F  I  K  A  K  K  D
C  L  A  S  S  R  O  O  M  L  B  S  N  A
F  R  I  E  N  D  S  L  E  P  E  N  S  L
K  Z  O  G  B  P  W  D  R  T  Q  P  F
T  E  A  C  H  E  R  E  I  G  E  U  Y  Z
O  U  P  A  P  E  R  R  K  Q  R  I  F  K
C  H  A  I  R  G  B  S  L  H  V  Z  H  E
```

ALPHABET	PENCIL
LUNCH	BOOKS
FRIENDS	MARKERS
TO LEARN	MATH
CLASSROOM	NUMBERS
LIBRARY	PAPER
FOLDERS	PENS
DESK	TEACHER
QUIZ	ANSWERS
EXAMS	CHAIR

36 - Adjetivos #2

```
W  S  P  I  C  Y  J  W  P  Q  U  H  J  U
X  C  R  E  A  T  I  V  E  Y  H  E  W  D
N  D  O  E  D  I  B  L  E  S  O  A  Z  L
L  D  D  R  A  M  A  T  I  C  S  L  N  O
X  S  U  T  N  L  K  O  H  Q  I  T  B  E
N  H  C  P  F  W  C  M  O  K  P  H  A  C
I  N  T  E  R  E  S  T  I  N  G  Y  M  R
D  E  I  L  E  O  S  N  O  R  M  A  L  H
R  W  V  E  S  J  U  T  A  S  A  L  T  Y
I  K  E  G  H  Q  M  D  R  T  I  R  E  D
D  R  Y  A  G  V  F  A  M  O  U  S  R  P
N  N  N  N  O  S  A  J  Y  T  N  R  P  U
L  E  O  T  F  G  W  U  O  S  D  G  A  I
D  E  S  C  R  I  P  T  I  V  E  U  M  L
```

TIRED	NATURAL
EDIBLE	NORMAL
CREATIVE	NEW
DESCRIPTIVE	PROUD
DRAMATIC	SPICY
ELEGANT	PRODUCTIVE
FAMOUS	SALTY
FRESH	HEALTHY
STRONG	DRY
INTERESTING	

37 - Cuerpo Humano

```
S  L  F  O  R  T  U  S  D  R  S  O  B  B
H  E  I  E  A  R  L  K  E  Q  U  P  H  R
O  G  N  S  J  T  N  O  S  E  X  C  I  A
U  O  G  Q  F  A  C  E  L  B  O  W  P  I
L  M  E  H  E  A  R  T  C  S  V  B  E  N
D  O  R  E  Y  E  B  R  D  K  K  N  E  E
E  U  P  A  B  S  L  U  H  I  W  X  L  E
R  T  P  D  T  L  J  O  A  N  K  L  E  M
Q  H  A  N  D  Z  O  K  T  O  N  G  U  E
C  B  Z  Q  Q  F  V  O  Q  Q  B  Q  D  J
Q  H  I  J  E  V  H  F  D  G  J  W  Z  F
P  S  I  Q  Q  C  A  T  V  F  F  W  I  I
H  W  M  N  N  Z  M  J  Q  L  O  K  L  Q
K  H  O  K  K  T  A  O  C  N  U  J  D  O
```

CHIN	TONGUE
MOUTH	HAND
HEAD	NOSE
FACE	EYE
BRAIN	EAR
ELBOW	SKIN
HEART	LEG
NECK	KNEE
FINGER	BLOOD
SHOULDER	ANKLE

38 - Ciencia

```
E L H Y P O T H E S I S H Z
Z X A L H F A C T E S Y F L
R S P B H M O L E C U L E S
M B E E O D X I W H E A O S
I Q I L R R F M E B Q P R C
E Z L W O I A A E C L L G I
M Z I F V E M T O P A A A E
P I E W T O J E O S G N N N
A H N V E O Y A N R T T I T
I S W E S D A T A T Y S S I
N A T U R E B O Z Q Y R M S
H T M P E A T M Z R C I V T
M E T H O D L P H Y S I C S
G R A V I T Y S F O S S I L
```

ATOM   HYPOTHESIS
SCIENTIST   LABORATORY
CLIMATE   METHOD
DATA   MINERALS
EXPERIMENT   MOLECULES
PHYSICS   NATURE
FOSSIL   ORGANISM
GRAVITY   PLANTS
FACT

39 - Dinosaurios

```
X D I S A P P E A R A N C E
L P R Z O O W O W I N G S T
N L M C P P T T W G M O I A
C A R N I V O R E E P I Z I
F R A P T O R R V M R X E L
O G V T M Z D E O A E F M T
S E E A R T H P L M H O U Z
S P N N X I F T U M I M V L
I R E N O E I I T O S N I Q
L E X C L R V L I T T I C U
S Y W Q I P M E O H O V I V
A T H V W E R O N N R O O W
S D K I H D S Y U T I R U H
H E R B I V O R E S C E S B
```

WINGS	MAMMOTH
CARNIVORE	OMNIVORE
TAIL	POWERFUL
DISAPPEARANCE	PREHISTORIC
ENORMOUS	PREY
SPECIES	RAPTOR
EVOLUTION	REPTILE
FOSSILS	SIZE
LARGE	EARTH
HERBIVORE	VICIOUS

40 - Restaurante #2

```
X A G F R U I T M O H A C S
U Y S O U P J W C H S C U P
D F N R M M W P P B A Y Y O
J I B K F G Z Q W A T E R O
H S N S P I C E S A L T R N
Y H B N B V V G M U I I S S
S C M Q E L U N C H H T J O
S H X Z V R K I T X V L E A
E E Z D E L I C I O U S E R
C H A I R J Y E G G S D U E
C R F R A P P E T I Z E R A
A A Y T G Q V I W E K H K P
R I K O E A U B A B X H O L
V E G E T A B L E S A L A D
```

WATER	FRUIT
LUNCH	ICE
APPETIZER	EGGS
BEVERAGE	CAKE
WAITER	FISH
DINNER	SALT
SPOON	CHAIR
DELICIOUS	SOUP
SALAD	FORK
SPICES	VEGETABLES

41 - Profesiones #1

```
M  P  F  M  B  A  N  K  E  R  M  J  A  D
V  L  I  U  P  I  A  N  I  S  T  E  S  O
N  U  R  S  E  D  E  L  E  X  H  W  T  C
H  M  E  I  G  Y  A  D  E  I  H  E  R  T
U  B  F  C  N  Z  Q  N  I  O  B  L  O  O
N  E  I  I  Q  P  N  N  C  T  C  E  N  R
T  R  G  A  Y  E  W  K  O  E  O  R  O  B
E  S  H  N  P  T  K  O  A  U  R  R  M  F
R  A  T  H  L  E  T  E  C  S  L  Q  E  Y
D  N  E  E  D  I  D  Q  H  R  T  Y  R  H
C  A  R  T  O  G  R  A  P  H  E  R  G  P
A  U  P  S  Y  C  H  O  L  O  G  I  S  T
H  A  M  B  A  S  S  A  D  O  R  W  T  B
P  N  D  K  G  E  O  L  O  G  I  S  T  G
```

ASTRONOMER	AMBASSADOR
ATHLETE	NURSE
DANCER	COACH
BANKER	PLUMBER
FIREFIGHTER	GEOLOGIST
CARTOGRAPHER	JEWELER
HUNTER	MUSICIAN
DOCTOR	PIANIST
EDITOR	PSYCHOLOGIST

42 - Vehículos

```
S P S U S V M U X L F J F S
H W S T I R E S Z E M J E U
U G T K R A F T F C B B R B
T S U B M A R I N E C H R W
T R H E L I C O P T E R Y A
L O A V Z R A T K Q W F Q Y
E C M B F P R B O N Q R Y E
X K B K U L L I T R A I N M
U E U A J A A C A R A V A N
P T L B M N E Y X D U H X Y
K O A U O E D C I E Z C Q W
B Y N S T A Q L C J O I K X
D Q C E O C T E W L Y H M Y
F V E Q R H W B Z T V T L C
```

AMBULANCE
BUS
AIRPLANE
RAFT
BOAT
BICYCLE
TRUCK
CARAVAN
CAR
ROCKET

FERRY
HELICOPTER
SHUTTLE
SUBWAY
MOTOR
TIRES
SUBMARINE
TAXI
TRACTOR
TRAIN

43 - Vacaciones #2

```
P  L  L  D  K  U  U  O  H  O  P  X  T  N
L  C  Q  B  E  A  C  H  Z  L  H  A  J  Y
V  S  S  S  T  S  F  S  P  X  O  V  L  Z
M  E  V  W  G  E  T  Z  G  O  T  I  E  M
H  A  J  S  N  K  M  I  E  W  O  S  I  O
J  O  U  R  N  E  Y  S  N  M  S  A  S  U
V  L  L  B  A  A  Z  L  T  A  V  Z  U  N
Y  P  T  I  G  L  E  A  R  P  T  A  R  T
A  P  E  A  D  G  I  N  A  X  U  I  E  A
X  U  N  N  X  A  J  D  I  T  S  R  O  I
H  O  T  E  L  I  Y  K  N  H  K  P  V  N
N  E  R  E  S  E  R  V  A  T  I  O  N  S
R  E  S  T  A  U  R  A  N  T  O  R  I  K
P  A  S  S  P  O  R  T  P  K  O  T  M  X
```

AIRPORT	PASSPORT
TENT	BEACH
DESTINATION	RESERVATIONS
PHOTOS	RESTAURANT
HOTEL	TAXI
ISLAND	TRAIN
MAP	HOLIDAY
SEA	JOURNEY
MOUNTAINS	VISA
LEISURE	

44 - Cumpleaños

```
M  L  E  Q  H  T  J  J  M  C  S  O  N  G
S  E  U  W  M  I  O  A  K  A  G  T  Q  L
E  P  M  N  W  M  Y  H  K  R  B  E  S  Z
M  Z  E  O  F  E  F  A  D  D  U  U  T  C
S  N  D  C  R  J  U  P  T  S  H  I  K  E
Y  Q  Z  S  I  I  L  P  A  R  T  Y  A  L
V  Q  H  X  E  A  E  Y  E  A  R  L  O  E
Z  C  A  X  N  D  L  S  Y  O  U  N  G  B
C  A  K  E  D  C  C  A  L  E  N  D  A  R
E  E  W  I  S  D  O  M  O  S  U  T  F  A
T  O  L  E  A  R  N  D  G  I  F  T  A  T
X  C  A  N  D  L  E  S  A  T  G  F  X  I
A  O  B  P  A  Z  N  W  A  Y  X  E  U  O
K  I  N  V  I  T  A  T  I  O  N  S  T  N
```

JOYFUL	INVITATIONS
FRIENDS	YOUNG
YEAR	PARTY
TO LEARN	CAKE
CALENDAR	MEMORIES
SONG	GIFT
CELEBRATION	WISDOM
DAY	CARDS
SPECIAL	TIME
HAPPY	CANDLES

45 - Baile

```
C R V E V M Y G P C P R C O
U H B X M U Z R O L S E U E
R Y O P O S F A S A Y H L V
L T D R V I J C T S W E T B
F H Y E E C O E U S G A U A
W M V S M O Z H R I S R R E
T L I S E W G Y E C S S E J
H Z S I N Y D R R A F A M P
N X U V T O T M A L N L O A
N X A E J U M P R P H F T R
C U L T U R A L T H H F I T
T R A D I T I O N A L Y O N
A C A D E M Y P U C Z I N E
J O Y F U L W H P T R N M R
```

ACADEMY
JOYFUL
ART
CLASSICAL
CHOREOGRAPHY
BODY
CULTURE
CULTURAL
EMOTION
REHEARSAL

EXPRESSIVE
GRACE
MOVEMENT
MUSIC
POSTURE
RHYTHM
JUMP
PARTNER
TRADITIONAL
VISUAL

46 - Matemáticas

```
A  R  I  H  M  E  T  I  C  O  L  Y  E
C  N  P  E  R  I  M  E  T  E  R  U  H  Q
C  T  G  G  J  R  S  P  H  E  R  E  M  U
D  R  B  L  A  Z  Y  Y  B  O  O  J  W  A
E  I  S  Z  E  G  E  O  M  E  T  R  Y  T
C  A  A  U  E  S  Y  B  H  M  X  H  W  I
I  N  P  M  P  A  R  A  L  L  E  L  L  O
M  G  L  M  E  X  P  O  N  E  N  T  D  N
A  L  R  E  C  T  A  N  G  L  E  L  R  H
L  E  U  L  Q  U  E  V  O  L  U  M  E  Y
P  O  L  Y  G  O  N  R  A  D  I  U  S  Y
C  I  R  C  U  M  F  E  R  E  N  C  E  O
P  E  R  P  E  N  D  I  C  U  L  A  R  I
P  A  R  A  L  L  E  L  O  G  R  A  M  Y
```

ARITHMETIC	PARALLELOGRAM
ANGLES	PERIMETER
CIRCUMFERENCE	PERPENDICULAR
DECIMAL	POLYGON
DIAMETER	RADIUS
EQUATION	RECTANGLE
SPHERE	SYMMETRY
EXPONENT	TRIANGLE
GEOMETRY	VOLUME
PARALLEL	

47 - Restaurante #1

```
T K M S A W C B O W L I J A
O N H Z L X A O R S A E S I
E I G S L I S I M E A F V N
A F T U E O H P T A A U T G
T E W Z R Z I L H R M D C R
M E N M G J E S B T E J X E
C N V Y Y K R I M E A S M D
C H I C K E N P L A T E S I
O S I C F V A M E N U Z A E
F P T J O Z P C Q R R U M N
F I F G O Z K I T C H E N T
E C X D D G I A E S F O R S
E Y L K I M N D E S S E R T
R R E S E R V A T I O N S W
```

ALLERGY	MENU
COFFEE	BREAD
CASHIER	SPICY
WAITRESS	PLATE
MEAT	CHICKEN
KITCHEN	DESSERT
TO EAT	RESERVATION
FOOD	SAUCE
KNIFE	NAPKIN
INGREDIENTS	BOWL

48 - Profesiones #2

```
B  P  G  P  A  I  N  T  E  R  E  M  O  Y
I  D  A  A  P  H  Y  S  I  C  I  A  N  E
O  A  S  T  R  O  N  A  U  T  C  P  D  D
L  I  H  X  W  D  E  T  E  C  T  I  V  E
O  W  U  E  D  B  E  T  L  O  T  L  M  N
G  N  I  B  X  W  O  N  E  U  P  O  V  T
I  N  V  E  N  T  O  R  E  A  O  T  I  I
S  E  N  G  I  N  E  E  R  R  C  E  H  S
T  J  O  U  R  N  A  L  I  S  T  H  K  T
H  J  W  P  H  I  L  O  S  O  P  H  E  R
X  S  U  R  G  E  O  N  C  U  D  V  V  R
L  I  N  G  U  I  S  T  H  D  L  C  N  E
I  L  L  U  S  T  R  A  T  O  R  E  O  S
P  H  O  T  O  G  R  A  P  H  E  R  T  N
```

ASTRONAUT	INVENTOR
BIOLOGIST	GARDENER
SURGEON	LINGUIST
DENTIST	PHYSICIAN
DETECTIVE	JOURNALIST
PHILOSOPHER	PILOT
PHOTOGRAPHER	PAINTER
ILLUSTRATOR	TEACHER
ENGINEER	

49 - Senderismo

```
C X I G O Q X A E H R Z O B
A S X I R K Z X D E P I X O
M L S O I C L I M A T E P O
P C F V E S L R O V C X R T
I M O U N T A I N Y S M E S
N A K P T C Y X F M Q O P U
G P F A A W V C V F Q S A M
Y Z W R T G W A T E R Q R M
M A Y K I N U N M F W U A I
F I S S O R A I S B I I T T
U V S U N Z J T D D L T I I
A N I M A L S M U E D O O R
J O Z Z K J H W T R S E N E
U O M C H H S T O N E S W D
```

CLIFF   MOUNTAIN
WATER   MOSQUITOES
ANIMALS   NATURE
BOOTS   ORIENTATION
CAMPING   PARKS
TIRED   HEAVY
CLIMATE   STONES
SUMMIT   PREPARATION
GUIDES   WILD
MAP   SUN

50 - Naturaleza

```
T O G L T W Y W K M N B I A
R O G M F O L I A G E R W R
O S M S O P G L J O O F R C
P H N P R R N D G T Z F P T
I E Q L E R O S I O N H D I
C L B S S A N C T U A R Y C
A T I E T S C Z D V N I N H
L E F R E S L E O J I V A G
B R O E U S O H F Z M E M L
A E G N R O U U L U A R I A
C Y A E J K D M C L L L C C
Z E O U C N S N P C S T P I
T T J U T D E S E R T I W E
V I T A L Y A H C D O N K R
```

BEES
ANIMALS
ARCTIC
BEAUTY
FOREST
DESERT
DYNAMIC
EROSION
FOLIAGE
GLACIER

FOG
CLOUDS
PEACEFUL
SHELTER
RIVER
WILD
SANCTUARY
SERENE
TROPICAL
VITAL

51 - Conduciendo

```
C W F K N G T U N N E L E M
V A J N T D R R D N V D M O
G R B B E B U S A J X P O T
M A P A S W C A N F E O T O
A R R V D T K F G E F L O R
C B X A P S P E E D R I R E
C A R O G M O T R R U C C D
I Q I A W E A Y H I G E Y H
D J O H K Q X E N D A U C Y
E G Y Y T E F U E L S E L V
N Q Z V X K S T R E E T E M
T L I C E N S E E J R T L R
L B C R P E D E S T R I A N
W S F G G B J M P L S O M P
```

ACCIDENT	MAP
BUS	MOTORCYCLE
STREET	MOTOR
TRUCK	PEDESTRIAN
CAR	DANGER
FUEL	POLICE
BRAKES	SAFETY
GARAGE	TRAFFIC
GAS	TUNNEL
LICENSE	SPEED

52 - Ballet

```
C F A B S K I L L R Y B M R
G A R R A E Q Y Y H Q M U E
D R C R T L V O T Y O U S H
Y S H M W I L F M T M S C E
P C O M P O S E R H K I L A
R M R W S K K T R M B C E R
A L E S S O N S I I R K S S
C C O O J R V T C C N I B A
T L G A P P L A U S E A D L
I Y R P J U O D A N C E R S
C B A U D I E N C E Z Y Z T
E X P R E S S I V E D W V Y
M Z H G E S T U R E M N B L
M E Y O R C H E S T R A A E
```

APPLAUSE
ARTISTIC
AUDIENCE
BALLERINA
DANCERS
COMPOSER
CHOREOGRAPHY
REHEARSAL
STYLE

EXPRESSIVE
GESTURE
SKILL
LESSONS
MUSCLES
MUSIC
ORCHESTRA
PRACTICE
RHYTHM

53 - Aventura

```
C B C N R W J Z Q E T P B D
I R O S I P O D Q X R R F O
S A F E T Y Y T D C A E L A
U V F E I A Q C X U V P X E
R E R K N C T M H R E A W G
P R I K E T L V O S L R N F
R Y E Y R I H M D I S A A A
I F N G A V U U P O A T T C
S W D O R I X N S N B I U H
I K S Y Y T O E U I E O R A
N V Z E G Y L W J S A N E N
G Q X D A N G E R O U S U C
N A V I G A T I O N T A M E
D I F F I C U L T Y Y X L X
```

ACTIVITY
JOY
FRIENDS
BEAUTY
DIFFICULTY
ENTHUSIASM
EXCURSION
UNUSUAL
ITINERARY
NATURE

NAVIGATION
NEW
CHANCE
DANGEROUS
PREPARATION
SAFETY
SURPRISING
BRAVERY
TRAVELS

54 - Pájaros

```
Q F V V N Q M S T O R K T G
L P O D O A A T W M G J O O
R E U Y M D U C K A N D U O
F L A M I N G O D C N W C S
Q I M P A V P Z W R K D A E
H C F H E P E U I O W I N P
P A L B G A N C H W F O A E
I N W O G R S P A R R O W
G S F K U R U L B L C D S Y
E E A U L O I X E H U S T Z
O L Y F L T N C M E C T R M
N U C H I C K E N R K V I F
I P H I T K Q O F O O M C M
W K B V A J T V H N O L H T
```

OSTRICH	SPARROW
EAGLE	HAWK
STORK	EGG
SWAN	PARROT
CUCKOO	PIGEON
CROW	DUCK
FLAMINGO	PELICAN
GOOSE	PENGUIN
HERON	CHICKEN
GULL	TOUCAN

55 - Surf

```
S  P  E  E  D  A  N  P  D  I  D  W  J  S
W  Y  H  A  K  J  U  M  I  M  Z  M  O  N
P  L  S  T  O  M  A  C  H  E  I  H  W  O
K  O  O  N  C  W  E  A  T  H  E  R  H  I
X  B  Y  P  E  X  T  R  E  M  E  Q  E  B
Z  Q  B  E  A  C  H  A  O  U  S  P  F  E
S  C  F  U  N  D  T  T  O  S  W  I  M  G
T  R  F  I  Z  Y  D  H  S  K  T  R  Q  I
R  O  O  W  A  J  T  L  B  P  Y  Y  R  N
E  W  A  V  E  O  R  E  E  F  R  B  L  N
N  D  M  N  T  D  X  T  P  H  C  A  Y  E
G  S  H  D  W  D  C  E  T  U  E  Y  Y  R
T  N  Y  P  B  J  P  O  P  U  L  A  R  F
H  C  H  A  M  P  I  O  N  A  X  Q  B  X
```

REEF	CROWDS
ATHLETE	TO SWIM
CHAMPION	OCEAN
WEATHER	WAVE
FUN	BEACH
FOAM	POPULAR
STYLE	BEGINNER
STOMACH	PADDLE
EXTREME	SPRAY
STRENGTH	SPEED

56 - Geografía

```
N R U S G A I S L A N D W F
C I T Y E P L B J Y P E O P
R I V E R A M T X V E X R P
M A P C C V O S I D S O L H
E B C K O U O R T C H D E
R X O O H L N U A E U S M M
I A U N F Z T T P T C D W I
D T N O A X A H I Y Y I E S
I L T R H W I V D N O K S P
A A R T A I N M T Q E X T H
N S Y H R E G I O N O N D E
L O N G I T U D E K K Y T R
L A T I T U D E S U D P G E
T E R R I T O R Y K N H V P
```

ALTITUDE   MERIDIAN
ATLAS   MOUNTAIN
CITY   WORLD
CONTINENT   NORTH
HEMISPHERE   WEST
ISLAND   COUNTRY
LATITUDE   REGION
LONGITUDE   RIVER
MAP   SOUTH
SEA   TERRITORY

57 - Deportes

```
U  G  B  R  R  W  H  O  C  K  E  Y  C  B
U  E  T  I  Q  F  I  J  F  F  L  K  H  A
Y  L  R  Y  C  C  I  N  E  M  F  Z  A  S
G  N  P  Q  Z  Y  M  R  N  D  P  M  M  K
P  L  A  Y  E  R  C  W  Y  E  S  O  P  E
R  G  E  R  L  G  O  L  R  B  R  V  I  T
T  O  S  W  I  M  A  T  E  A  A  E  O  B
X  O  T  E  A  M  C  E  F  S  T  M  N  A
K  U  A  F  Q  K  H  N  E  E  H  E  S  L
H  I  D  E  T  R  G  N  R  B  L  N  H  L
G  W  I  C  F  B  O  I  E  A  E  T  I  M
L  A  U  Y  Y  J  L  S  E  L  T  O  P  Q
R  O  M  N  Z  O  F  S  M  L  E  L  O  U
G  A  P  E  G  Y  M  N  A  S  I  U  M  X
```

ATHLETE	WINNER
REFEREE	GYMNASIUM
BASKETBALL	GOLF
BASEBALL	HOCKEY
BICYCLE	GAME
CHAMPIONSHIP	PLAYER
COACH	MOVEMENT
TEAM	TO SWIM
STADIUM	TENNIS

58 - Actividades

```
E  H  C  E  R  A  M  I  C  S  C  B  F  H
N  P  U  Z  Z  L  E  S  P  U  R  L  F  V
G  T  R  N  Q  K  L  S  A  M  A  G  I  C
X  A  D  E  T  B  Z  O  I  P  F  H  S  G
E  U  Q  Z  A  I  L  V  N  L  T  I  H  A
E  D  Z  A  S  D  N  E  T  E  S  K  I  R
G  A  M  E  S  H  I  G  I  A  P  I  N  D
X  C  W  L  K  Y  T  N  N  S  B  N  G  E
M  T  D  A  I  A  R  T  G  U  U  G  Z  N
T  I  U  D  L  Z  P  M  Q  R  I  R  S  I
R  V  M  O  L  F  I  C  U  E  E  K  E  N
B  I  P  H  O  T  O  G  R  A  P  H  Y  G
Y  T  D  C  G  S  S  E  W  I  N  G  U  G
Z  Y  I  N  T  E  R  E  S  T  S  O  D  N
```

ACTIVITY	GAMES
ART	READING
CRAFTS	MAGIC
HUNTING	LEISURE
CERAMICS	FISHING
SEWING	PAINTING
PHOTOGRAPHY	PLEASURE
SKILL	PUZZLES
INTERESTS	HIKING
GARDENING	

59 - Verduras

```
B  J  Q  D  A  U  Q  S  A  I  Z  P  L  N
E  D  M  R  K  M  N  P  E  J  Q  U  E  C
K  J  D  T  U  R  N  I  P  U  K  A  J  A
P  A  R  S  L  E  Y  N  R  A  D  I  S  H
G  I  N  G  E  R  P  A  S  B  F  B  X  G
M  P  O  T  A  T  O  C  E  L  E  R  Y  A
S  U  E  S  D  V  H  H  O  N  I  O  N  R
A  M  S  G  O  N  Q  D  Z  T  H  C  Y  L
L  P  Q  H  G  K  M  E  I  O  W  C  E  I
A  K  A  S  R  P  O  D  S  M  A  O  B  C
D  I  R  P  B  O  L  J  F  A  B  L  Q  Z
E  N  H  V  Q  D  O  A  Z  T  N  I  J  B
O  L  I  V  E  S  M  M  N  O  X  F  K  H
C  U  C  U  M  B  E  R  J  T  F  F  C  O
```

GARLIC	GINGER
CELERY	TURNIP
EGGPLANT	OLIVE
BROCCOLI	POTATO
PUMPKIN	CUCUMBER
ONION	PARSLEY
SALAD	RADISH
SPINACH	MUSHROOM
PEA	TOMATO

60 - Instrumentos Musicales

```
S A X O P H O N E O F B G M
I F E X F H Y Z P Z Y A U A
V I O L I N M L E G J N I N
B A S S O O N Q R H U J T D
C L A R I N E T C M A O A O
T R U M P E T S U N C R R L
Q Q O R F S P T S D E Y P I
H B O T N S G Z S J L F Q N
E Y Q X J I R P I F L U T E
M A R I M B A I O B O E S G
D W R D G R C A N U R P T O
R S H A R M O N I C A R Y N
U H G B C T R O M B O N E G
M N A E T A M B O U R I N E
```

HARMONICA	OBOE
HARP	TAMBOURINE
BANJO	PERCUSSION
CLARINET	PIANO
BASSOON	SAXOPHONE
FLUTE	DRUM
GONG	TROMBONE
GUITAR	TRUMPET
MANDOLIN	VIOLIN
MARIMBA	CELLO

61 - Escalada

```
N  R  P  C  H  I  K  I  N  G  G  P  Y  Z
P  X  G  R  U  G  U  I  D  E  S  H  N  E
I  I  N  J  U  R  Y  B  C  M  B  Y  G  H
G  L  O  V  E  S  I  O  C  E  U  S  C  V
J  K  F  N  A  R  R  O  W  L  B  I  R  A
T  Z  U  J  Y  F  X  T  S  N  C  C  U  S
Q  X  L  O  Y  A  N  S  D  I  M  A  P  T
A  T  M  O  S  P  H  E  R  E  T  L  B  R
S  T  A  B  I  L  I  T  Y  W  N  Y  G  E
A  L  T  I  T  U  D  E  X  P  E  R  T  N
H  N  C  L  I  L  T  R  A  I  N  I  N  G
P  R  D  A  H  E  L  M  E  T  X  N  Y  T
G  H  G  I  V  T  E  R  R  A  I  N  C  H
U  W  M  E  G  E  Y  O  S  Q  M  G  K  C
```

ALTITUDE	PHYSICAL
ATMOSPHERE	TRAINING
BOOTS	STRENGTH
HELMET	GLOVES
CAVE	GUIDES
CURIOSITY	INJURY
STABILITY	MAP
NARROW	HIKING
EXPERT	TERRAIN

62 - Mascotas

```
H  V  I  F  O  P  Y  Q  L  J  G  D  U  B
A  R  J  P  F  D  O  G  E  H  V  J  T  Q
M  G  O  A  T  I  R  H  A  G  M  Q  T  T
S  C  B  R  X  V  S  S  S  F  U  I  A  U
T  L  T  R  X  P  K  H  H  P  U  P  P  Y
E  A  C  O  W  A  T  E  R  A  B  B  I  T
R  W  A  T  U  R  T  L  E  W  E  F  K  R
L  S  T  A  K  W  X  S  K  S  R  C  J  I
K  I  M  I  V  I  M  U  U  S  S  T  C  C
Z  A  Z  L  J  R  B  N  B  L  Z  U  L  L
K  B  A  A  F  M  O  U  S  E  F  A  H  N
Y  T  G  Y  R  O  C  O  L  L  A  R  M  S
P  V  V  H  R  D  O  H  K  O  W  N  W  M
B  I  P  R  M  S  X  D  C  L  H  Y  U  R
```

WATER	HAMSTER
GOAT	LIZARD
PUPPY	PARROT
TAIL	PAWS
COLLAR	DOG
FOOD	FISH
RABBIT	MOUSE
LEASH	TURTLE
CLAWS	COW
CAT	

63 - Formas

```
Z  S  U  L  P  H  X  F  C  C  O  N  E  L
A  N  P  Z  O  Y  N  F  O  U  C  P  N  S
E  D  G  E  S  P  Q  F  R  R  I  U  I  G
S  I  D  E  Q  E  A  A  N  V  R  U  B  O
T  E  O  L  U  R  R  K  E  E  C  Y  A  E
F  M  V  R  A  B  C  T  R  U  L  B  C  D
P  X  A  X  R  O  S  R  T  D  E  P  C  W
R  O  L  K  E  L  P  Y  R  A  M  I  D  E
I  D  L  L  C  A  H  L  I  N  E  U  X  L
S  K  N  Y  J  K  E  C  A  J  I  S  G  L
M  L  Z  M  G  N  R  W  N  L  E  O  Z  I
N  C  P  L  B  O  E  O  G  W  L  M  C  P
Z  R  E  C  T  A  N  G  L  E  K  A  B  S
C  Y  L  I  N  D  E  R  E  P  N  L  R  E
```

ARC	CORNER
EDGES	HYPERBOLA
CYLINDER	SIDE
CIRCLE	LINE
CONE	OVAL
SQUARE	PYRAMID
CUBE	POLYGON
CURVE	PRISM
ELLIPSE	RECTANGLE
SPHERE	TRIANGLE

64 - Flores

```
D A I S Y V B J J R J G P L
A A J W A L R E A R J J E I
N C F Z L G K D S A E I T L
D A V F B A X U M P L E A A
E L C Z O R C H I D A I L C
L E L G U D M E N K V X L S
I N E M Q E I C E P E O N Y
O D I A U N C L C O N D I Y
N U V G E I N O L P D G Y L
L L V N T A I V N P E H T N
N A R O S E K E C Y R L Y V
Q D W L G A V R T U L I P K
H I B I S C U S V Q O B K T
W H J A S U N F L O W E R E
```

POPPY

CALENDULA

DANDELION

GARDENIA

SUNFLOWER

HIBISCUS

JASMINE

LAVENDER

LILAC

LILY

MAGNOLIA

DAISY

DAFFODIL

ORCHID

PEONY

PETAL

BOUQUET

ROSE

CLOVER

TULIP

65 - Astronomía

```
D V G P L A N E T E O C A S
T L A A A N A Y T C B O S U
T E L E S C O P E L S N T P
P M A C Y C Y G J I E S R E
V E X P F L L E A P R T O R
A T Y S K Y X Y S S V E N N
S E A R T H G F T E A L O O
T O C O S M O S R A T L M V
E R A D I A T I O N O A E A
R N O S I I U Y N S R T R C
O Q J C E I F H A H Y I Y T
I N W I K G E Q U I N O X R
D R Q P I E I S T P H N Q N
C N X O R Y T M O O N K J Z
```

ASTEROID   GALAXY
ASTRONAUT   MOON
ASTRONOMER   METEOR
SKY   OBSERVATORY
ROCKET   PLANET
CONSTELLATION   RADIATION
COSMOS   SUPERNOVA
ECLIPSE   TELESCOPE
EQUINOX   EARTH

66 - Tiempo

```
M E W L S L Y M I I W D V C
N O W Q F N C E N T U R Y A
M J N I G H T C A R Q D S L
V O E T W E E K V R N R R E
U U M N H O U R F O Z W E N
P V D E S F N O O N D A Y D
M T A N N U A L D U K B U A
Y I Y E S T E R D A Y T X R
H S Q L R U I P A C L O C K
B W I S H R K F O X H D A D
B E F O R E W C X H T A L M
Q P G D P W S E B W H Y W P
Y P X D E C A D E U R T X S
M I N U T E M O R N I N G E
```

NOW
BEFORE
ANNUAL
YEAR
YESTERDAY
CALENDAR
DECADE
DAY
FUTURE
HOUR

TODAY
MORNING
NOON
MONTH
MINUTE
MOMENT
NIGHT
CLOCK
WEEK
CENTURY

67 - Paisajes

```
G L A C I E R T V D H O H V
J D N A S E A O B E A C H E
E H V V L W O B Y S Z L J D
G S Y E A L A K E E S F L W
L E T X N N S M Y R W S X J
A J Y U D Y I Q P T W U Q P
G D Z S A N S S E U A V D O
O R I V E R M O U N T A I N
O O J M H R Y P O D E L C H
N V O L C A N O E R R L E N
P E N I N S U L A A F E B B
L X L Q X T S R L Q A Y E B
E T U T G S D E I B L C R E
I F X W P I B F Z G L S G G
```

WATERFALL	SEA
CAVE	MOUNTAIN
DESERT	OASIS
ESTUARY	SWAMP
GEYSER	PENINSULA
GLACIER	BEACH
ICEBERG	RIVER
ISLAND	TUNDRA
LAKE	VALLEY
LAGOON	VOLCANO

68 - Días y Meses

```
S  M  O  N  D  A  Y  X  D  F  N  F  J  T
E  A  C  S  T  U  E  S  D  A  Y  R  A  H
P  U  T  F  E  B  R  U  A  R  Y  I  N  U
T  F  O  U  E  D  Q  N  A  K  F  D  U  R
E  W  B  E  R  T  Z  D  U  P  I  A  A  S
M  E  E  N  Q  D  E  A  G  B  R  Y  R  D
B  D  R  O  Z  W  A  Y  U  Q  B  I  Y  A
E  N  Y  V  J  J  E  Y  S  M  P  M  L  Y
R  E  D  E  B  U  F  E  T  O  J  U  L  Y
C  S  Z  M  L  N  Z  A  K  N  W  D  L  B
O  D  Z  B  D  E  U  R  F  T  M  I  B  T
C  A  L  E  N  D  A  R  V  H  G  D  B  L
F  Y  F  R  F  Z  K  I  H  U  D  B  M  S
Y  Z  E  H  I  P  M  E  H  R  G  O  O  X
```

APRIL	MONDAY
AUGUST	TUESDAY
YEAR	MONTH
CALENDAR	WEDNESDAY
SUNDAY	NOVEMBER
JANUARY	OCTOBER
FEBRUARY	SATURDAY
THURSDAY	WEEK
JULY	SEPTEMBER
JUNE	FRIDAY

69 - Chocolate

```
Q X A R O M A P V R S M A K
Q U C R T Q X B O S U G A R
F I A Y T B M V J W I A N D
L N R L M I H N S E D Z W E
A G A F I T S C K E U E K L
V R M A A T I A D T Y P R I
O E E V J E Y L N F W T Y C
R D L O O R R O C A C A O I
R I S R J H J R O Q L E O O
E E O I V W F I C T Q X G U
C N Y T Q Z R E O A Y O O S
I T Y E I I J S N S Q T R C
P E A N U T S O U T G I Y U
E U P H Q K T U T E V C T E
```

BITTER
AROMA
ARTISANAL
SUGAR
PEANUTS
CACAO
QUALITY
CALORIES
CARAMEL
COCONUT

DELICIOUS
SWEET
EXOTIC
FAVORITE
TASTE
INGREDIENT
POWDER
RECIPE
FLAVOR

70 - Barbacoas

```
C H I L D R E N F I C G F H
H O U E N L O A O A C H I V
I T O M A T O E S W M Z Q O
C F J A P Y L B A O E I L R
K W H L D Z A I A N D V L P
E F R U I T M U S I C E L Y
N H T N N K T N A O R G Y U
S S F C N G P U L N J E L T
U A A H E A E G A S A T K N
M U C L R M P R D C W A S K
M C P E T E P I S Y J B A B
E E B I X S E L I A C L X R
R H L D X X R L A G K E B R
A F W X K N I V E S G S J H
```

LUNCH
HOT
ONIONS
DINNER
KNIVES
SALADS
FAMILY
FRUIT
HUNGER
GAMES

MUSIC
CHILDREN
GRILL
PEPPER
CHICKEN
SALT
SAUCE
TOMATOES
SUMMER
VEGETABLES

71 - Ropa

```
G S O M U N M S P S I U N J
M Z C P B E P H G A F M H W
Q A W A P V D I O N Z B J J
A L J X R S V R E D U L A E
G B Z C O F F T W A X O C W
J B N R A P R O N L H U K E
P A N T S B K E C S B S E L
F S P I S X J W O Q J E T R
A E W Y W P M K A L Y A L Y
S S U H E A X D T G V B D T
H H B P A J A M A S K I R T
I O S P T T G I G L O V E S
O E A N E C K L A C E B S W
N Z Z B R A C E L E T C S P
```

COAT
BLOUSE
SCARF
SHIRT
JACKET
BELT
NECKLACE
APRON
SKIRT
GLOVES

JEWELRY
FASHION
PANTS
PAJAMAS
BRACELET
SANDALS
HAT
SWEATER
DRESS
SHOE

72 - Meditación

```
M  N  A  K  I  N  D  N  E  S  S  S  Q  Q
O  J  I  C  A  L  M  U  S  I  C  G  I  E
V  T  P  R  C  L  A  R  I  T  Y  R  P  O
E  P  H  S  Q  E  P  P  M  O  Y  A  O  B
M  E  C  O  E  E  P  V  K  C  K  T  S  S
E  R  O  B  U  N  A  T  U  R  E  I  T  E
N  S  M  Q  R  G  C  A  A  V  F  T  U  R
T  P  P  W  D  E  H  N  B  N  E  U  R  V
P  E  A  C  E  M  A  T  M  N  C  D  E  A
G  C  S  H  C  E  B  T  S  B  L  E  X  T
O  T  S  V  G  N  P  M  H  P  F  C  E  I
X  I  I  C  H  T  N  I  E  I  C  Q  A  O
P  V  O  Z  N  A  N  N  B  J  N  M  R  N
W  E  N  E  O  L  E  D  T  I  W  G  Q  L
```

ACCEPTANCE   MUSIC
KINDNESS   NATURE
CALM   OBSERVATION
CLARITY   PEACE
COMPASSION   THOUGHTS
GRATITUDE   PERSPECTIVE
MENTAL   POSTURE
MIND   BREATHING
MOVEMENT

73 - Libros

```
Q J N V I H E Z A Y S P A H
R E A D E R U Z P M T O U N
E F R W P O E M M K O E T V
L Q R I A S Y A O C R T H W
E E A N G D E P J R Y R O R
V L T F E B V R K A O Y R I
A F O O P D Q E I C E U H T
N H R B N L X C N E H O S T
T D U A L I T Y A T S R O E
C O L L E C T I O N U Q O N
I N V E N T I V E O F R Z Q
T R A G I C V D V V Y Z E P
D M G P U C O N T E X T T R
L I T E R A R Y I L D O P O
```

AUTHOR	LITERARY
ADVENTURE	NARRATOR
COLLECTION	NOVEL
CONTEXT	PAGE
DUALITY	RELEVANT
WRITTEN	POEM
STORY	POETRY
HUMOROUS	SERIES
INVENTIVE	TRAGIC
READER	

74 - Nutrición

```
Q U R B M Q C C L Q K C D X
U A R Q Y Y E Z E D I B L E
A N P H X N N U T R I E N T
L H G P H T K Q F J E C B F
I D I G E S T I O N P A A B
T R R I A T D C T F R L L O
Y W S V L I I M Z L O O A S
H W E Q T P E T D A T R N B
O F N I H B T P E V E I C I
N D M L G S D C N O I E E T
S A U C E H T M Q R N S D T
T O X I N D T R M Y S Q P E
C A R B O H Y D R A T E S R
F E R M E N T A T I O N O S
```

BITTER   BALANCED
APPETITE   FERMENTATION
QUALITY   NUTRIENT
CALORIES   WEIGHT
CARBOHYDRATES   PROTEINS
CEREALS   FLAVOR
EDIBLE   SAUCE
DIET   HEALTH
DIGESTION   TOXIN

75 - Bondad

```
O C P I H H A J R B O H T H
F H A P P Y O O E T W E O O
G R T R O R T N C S I L L S
E F I G E N T L E J J P E P
N Q E E T K W S P S U F R I
U J N N N V V Y T T T U A T
I Q T E X D M U I D I L N A
N G L R Y L L O V I N G T B
E X Q O V W L Y E T R H R L
S Z F U A T T E N T I V E E
D R E S P E C T F U L X H W
C O M P A S S I O N A T E L
A F F E C T I O N A T E N I
R E L I A B L E A Y Y D J J
```

AFFECTIONATE   HONEST
FRIENDLY   HOSPITABLE
LOVING   PATIENT
ATTENTIVE   RECEPTIVE
COMPASSIONATE   RESPECTFUL
HAPPY   GENTLE
RELIABLE   TOLERANT
GENEROUS   HELPFUL
GENUINE

76 - Edificios

```
A  P  A  R  T  M  E  N  T  H  J  L  O  O
H  O  T  E  L  F  A  C  T  O  R  Y  Y  B
T  O  W  E  R  S  A  C  A  S  T  L  E  S
G  C  M  L  F  V  F  I  K  P  D  G  U  E
P  X  J  P  X  A  T  D  P  I  W  P  N  R
S  F  Q  Q  D  D  R  U  R  T  Z  K  I  V
T  C  I  N  E  M  A  M  G  A  D  B  V  A
A  H  H  Y  B  Y  L  W  G  L  U  A  E  T
D  E  E  O  E  M  B  A  S  S  Y  R  R  O
I  I  H  A  O  G  A  R  A  G  E  N  S  R
U  J  J  B  T  L  H  O  S  T  E  L  I  Y
M  N  V  I  J  E  M  U  S  E  U  M  T  T
P  D  L  A  B  O  R  A  T  O  R  Y  Y  G
S  U  P  E  R  M  A  R  K  E  T  M  D  S
```

HOSTEL	FARM
APARTMENT	HOSPITAL
CASTLE	HOTEL
CINEMA	LABORATORY
EMBASSY	MUSEUM
SCHOOL	OBSERVATORY
STADIUM	SUPERMARKET
FACTORY	THEATER
GARAGE	TOWER
BARN	UNIVERSITY

77 - Océano

```
J E L L Y F I S H Y B O A T
E E L K D A F P O P D C X U
W H A L E Z V O O Y S T E R
K L C S C C K N Y G H O B T
E S L Q C C R G V B A P I L
A H H C F O R E E F R U K E
S R X Q D R S A L T K S A U
Y I G W G A P C B F U J U S
N M S D O L P H I N I N P L
W P A L G A E W K A F S A H
P K Y T I D E S Y X O T H Y
P J J F L X L P E P I O W S
J R Q Q V V B Q W G Q R X O
Q L K J E T L B P A W M G O
```

ALGAE
EEL
REEF
TUNA
WHALE
BOAT
SHRIMP
CRAB
CORAL
DOLPHIN

SPONGE
TIDES
JELLYFISH
OYSTER
FISH
OCTOPUS
SALT
SHARK
STORM
TURTLE

78 - Ciudad

```
A  F  L  K  G  F  M  A  R  K  E  T  F  N
V  I  F  M  C  Q  U  S  S  U  Z  J  Z  I
W  T  R  Z  W  P  S  B  A  N  K  Z  Y  K
C  I  F  P  U  H  E  V  C  I  N  E  M  A
S  L  Z  O  O  A  U  R  M  V  H  D  V  S
T  S  I  D  N  R  M  T  H  E  A  T  E  R
A  C  X  N  H  M  T  W  O  R  H  H  A  Y
D  H  O  C  I  A  G  D  T  S  T  O  R  E
I  O  Z  H  N  C  B  D  E  I  Z  Z  X  W
U  O  K  J  O  Y  G  A  L  T  A  P  J  P
M  L  I  B  R  A  R  Y  K  Y  A  Y  C  M
S  U  P  E  R  M  A  R  K  E  T  A  C  G
K  Y  A  G  A  L  L  E  R  Y  R  X  B  W
N  F  L  O  R  I  S  T  S  B  D  Y  R  Q
```

AIRPORT
BANK
LIBRARY
CINEMA
CLINIC
SCHOOL
STADIUM
PHARMACY
FLORIST
GALLERY

HOTEL
MARKET
MUSEUM
BAKERY
SUPERMARKET
THEATER
STORE
UNIVERSITY
ZOO

79 - Conservación

```
R  R  C  P  G  R  E  E  N  L  E  I  E  T
E  I  Y  U  O  R  G  A  N  I  C  M  N  J
D  X  C  E  F  L  V  O  B  S  P  H  V  C
U  M  L  J  D  U  L  S  F  G  Z  E  I  L
C  V  E  C  W  H  U  U  S  N  K  A  R  I
E  G  E  C  O  S  Y  S  T  E  M  L  O  M
D  H  A  B  I  T  A  T  G  I  N  T  N  A
U  K  N  G  R  R  A  A  G  K  O  H  M  T
C  H  A  N  G  E  S  I  F  Q  G  N  E  E
A  C  T  G  R  C  R  N  W  G  A  W  N  E
T  K  U  V  C  Y  L  A  W  A  O  N  T  R
I  L  R  A  F  C  V  B  R  P  T  C  A  B
O  D  A  H  H  L  X  L  X  N  C  E  L  R
N  U  L  J  D  E  I  E  O  H  S  U  R  Y
```

WATER
ENVIRONMENTAL
CHANGES
CYCLE
CLIMATE
POLLUTION
ECOSYSTEM
EDUCATION

HABITAT
NATURAL
ORGANIC
RECYCLE
REDUCE
HEALTH
SUSTAINABLE
GREEN

80 - Exploración

```
A I A E D E N C X L C X D L
T C E X H A U S T I O N I A
R D T C U L T U R E S E S N
A G O I A N I M A L S P C G
V U A T V Q A O W I L D O U
E N P E R I L O U S T U V A
L K H M D B T K O W W H E G
C N J E U K C Y R T I U R E
X O Q N T O L E A R N I Y O
X W U T S P A C E G E J Z R
U N E R V K S L P K W W P R
D I S T A N T T E R R A I N
Y L T N D G L K D X S F S H
Y H K I T U E A F S H V E X
```

ACTIVITY
EXHAUSTION
ANIMALS
TO LEARN
QUEST
COURAGE
CULTURES
UNKNOWN
DISCOVERY

DISTANT
EXCITEMENT
SPACE
LANGUAGE
NEW
PERILOUS
WILD
TERRAIN
TRAVEL

81 - Campeonato

```
S  T  O  B  R  E  A  T  H  E  F  D  G  V
J  O  C  H  A  M  P  I  O  N  S  H  I  P
E  U  P  E  R  F  O  R  M  A  N  C  E  J
N  R  D  V  I  C  T  O  R  Y  X  R  Z  O
D  N  G  G  A  M  E  S  G  I  Z  K  D  F
U  A  C  K  E  L  E  A  G  U  E  R  J  I
R  M  P  E  R  S  P  I  R  A  T  I  O  N
A  E  E  Y  O  R  S  D  R  Z  B  V  R  A
N  N  E  D  H  E  E  P  C  Z  W  I  O  L
C  T  T  E  A  M  V  S  O  T  X  Q  X  I
E  M  B  G  N  L  K  X  A  R  R  A  R  S
S  T  R  A  T  E  G  Y  C  X  T  K  N  T
C  H  A  M  P  I  O  N  H  O  D  S  A  Y
H  H  U  M  O  T  I  V  A  T  I  O  N  J
```

CHAMPIONSHIP	LEAGUE
CHAMPION	MEDAL
SPORTS	MOTIVATION
COACH	PERFORMANCE
TEAM	ENDURANCE
STRATEGY	TO BREATHE
FINALIST	TOURNAMENT
GAMES	PERSPIRATION
JUDGE	VICTORY

82 - Actividades y Ocio

```
G A R D E N I N G Z U S C B
N O C H R Y J Z H D J H V A
W H A T E N N I S P Q O U S
N I M A L R A P H B B P V K
E K P U A L A R T U O P E E
M I I K X V B C P G X I H T
F N N N I K X D I V I N G B
I G G F N E F J A N N G T A
S T U O G D O S C O G E Z L
H R T B S W I M M I N G P L
I A G O L F B A S E B A L L
N V S O C C E R X Y T K P Q
G E S U R F I N G L L J H E
L L P A I N T I N G U K Y Z
```

ART   GARDENING
BASKETBALL   SWIMMING
BASEBALL   FISHING
BOXING   PAINTING
DIVING   RELAXING
CAMPING   HIKING
RACING   SURFING
SHOPPING   TENNIS
SOCCER   TRAVEL
GOLF

83 - Comida #1

```
O U Q E H I B M R T K G S V
S N P F W A A J E E I W A M
J P H Q S E R M F A H S L M
P U I G A R L I C Z T T T O
M C I N F L E M O N M R J O
Y E N C A H Y I S M C A Z C
U S T B E C J L K I A W B I
J O N I O N H K O N R B A N
T U R N I P E A R T R E S N
W P S U G A R J G U O R I A
G T Z M A B Y S V N T R L M
F X M W K A S A L A D Y S O
E W P B K U G Z N V K H K N
P N R O R V Y D L O C M B E
```

GARLIC
BASIL
TUNA
SUGAR
CINNAMON
MEAT
BARLEY
ONION
SALAD
SPINACH

STRAWBERRY
JUICE
MILK
LEMON
MINT
TURNIP
PEAR
SALT
SOUP
CARROT

84 - Virtudes #1

```
I  N  D  E  P  E  N  D  E  N  T  L  I  E
P  Y  P  A  S  S  I  O  N  A  T  E  K  D
L  A  I  M  A  G  I  N  A  T  I  V  E  V
A  R  T  I  S  T  I  C  D  Z  F  Z  P  J
M  E  G  I  I  F  H  E  L  P  F  U  L  I
O  L  E  C  E  U  F  Q  E  L  N  N  F  B
D  I  N  L  F  N  D  E  C  I  S  I  V  E
E  A  E  E  N  T  C  U  R  I  O  U  S
S  B  R  A  I  Y  G  O  O  D  F  Y  R  G
T  L  O  N  C  P  I  Q  G  Z  Z  E  B  U
Q  E  U  W  I  S  E  C  H  O  F  J  Z  M
B  I  S  X  E  P  R  A  C  T  I  C  A  L
H  U  R  I  N  T  E  L  L  I  G  E  N  T
D  F  J  R  T  C  H  A  R  M  I  N  G  W
```

PASSIONATE	IMAGINATIVE
ARTISTIC	INDEPENDENT
GOOD	INTELLIGENT
CURIOUS	CLEAN
DECISIVE	MODEST
EFFICIENT	PATIENT
CHARMING	PRACTICAL
RELIABLE	WISE
GENEROUS	HELPFUL
FUNNY	

85 - Literatura

```
A T F M E T A P H O R S Z A
U R I K G P O E T I C T A N
T A C C H B O U D J F Y N A
H G T H E M E E R C M L A L
O E I M W X Z R M Z A E L O
R D O B B I O G R A P H Y G
P Y N O V E L R G H O F S Y
N A R R A T O R H U Y D I U
Y K K L N U G S W Y Q T S F
F W T R F C M D T C M I H Z
C O M P A R I S O N H E W M
C O N C L U S I O N X V S W
A N E C D O T E L G Z G A I
M D I A L O G U E T F H F R
```

ANALOGY
ANALYSIS
ANECDOTE
AUTHOR
BIOGRAPHY
COMPARISON
CONCLUSION
DIALOGUE
STYLE
FICTION

METAPHOR
NARRATOR
NOVEL
POEM
POETIC
RHYME
RHYTHM
THEME
TRAGEDY

86 - Clima

```
T C L O U D R Y F S C F S H
S L Y I A Q V D I P L O F L
P T K U G C P S Q C I P L Q
S E O N W H Q W U I M F O G
K M V N D U T I P A A F O T
Y P O L A R T N C P T W D O
T E S A U R H D I E E I O R
W R T T N I U M O N S O O N
U A O I C C N D V X G D Y A
L T R G D A D Q O Q X R R D
G U M Z F N E Z G T Q H J O
B R E E Z E R D R O U G H T
Q E M A T M O S P H E R E N
T R O P I C A L V R F X D P
```

ATMOSPHERE
BREEZE
SKY
CLIMATE
ICE
HURRICANE
FLOOD
MONSOON
FOG
CLOUD

POLAR
LIGHTNING
DRY
DROUGHT
TEMPERATURE
STORM
TORNADO
TROPICAL
THUNDER
WIND

87 - Comida #2

```
R S B C S B C W V Z F Q C G
R I C E D K H B H S J U H R
K I W I D Y O C H E E S E A
G O J B S F C Y A Z A R R P
A R T I C H O K E C E T R E
T K H B E C L E M U G F Y S
U O C A L H A P P L E M E U
E B H N E I T X T R Y K G N
A R T A R C E J O K O C G F
W L U N Y K Q J M Y G E P L
H S M A I E M D A D U G L O
M S M O O N V O T S R G A W
Q M G I N G E R O L T Q N E
L O R J Q D Q B R E A D T R
```

ARTICHOKE
ALMOND
CELERY
RICE
EGGPLANT
CHERRY
CHOCOLATE
SUNFLOWER
EGG
GINGER

KIWI
APPLE
BREAD
BANANA
CHICKEN
CHEESE
TOMATO
WHEAT
GRAPE
YOGURT

88 - Castillos

```
D C T S W O R D Y N A S T Y
R A F O P R I N C E S S E D
A T E R W A K I N G D O M H
G A U P D E L S H I E L D O
O P D X D L R A A R M O R R
N U A Q X T H Y C Q K J B S
U L L H P C J X N E U C U E
E T L U U N I C O R N H W W
C R O W N N Y O I V E O E N
F O R T R E S S H E M E N D
P R I N C E W W Y Q P R M X
G P K E O M U A K N I G H T
Y F M A R F N Z L J R Y S F
Y D V B N Q N O B L E N A O
```

ARMOR
KNIGHT
HORSE
CATAPULT
CROWN
DYNASTY
DRAGON
SHIELD
SWORD
FEUDAL

FORTRESS
EMPIRE
NOBLE
PALACE
WALL
PRINCESS
PRINCE
KINGDOM
TOWER
UNICORN

89 - Arte

```
P O H I P E R S O N A L S V
O R F M N W J X U T F S G I
R I I C J S U C J B U D Q S
T G G C J Y P S N T J Z L U
R I U X O M S I M P L E C A
A N R X S B J D R K G C C L
Y A E Y Q O Q C S E W A P T
C L H G G L M M O O D Z T D
H E X P R E S S I O N D Q V
O C R Q S Z P C O M P L E X
N G Y A S U R R E A L I S M
E Y E I M P A I N T I N G S
S A G M M I P O E T R Y S J
T G Z H D J C R E A T E R S
```

CERAMIC   PERSONAL
COMPLEX   PAINTINGS
CREATE   POETRY
EXPRESSION   PORTRAY
FIGURE   SIMPLE
HONEST   SYMBOL
MOOD   SURREALISM
INSPIRED   SUBJECT
ORIGINAL   VISUAL

90 - Herboristería

```
T  C  G  R  E  E  N  A  T  R  C  P  I  R
G  U  O  Q  H  A  U  R  A  C  R  A  N  O
N  L  N  M  A  R  J  O  R  A  M  R  G  S
Q  I  T  G  D  R  W  M  R  N  H  S  R  E
U  N  E  C  I  X  D  A  A  D  C  L  E  M
A  A  S  C  L  R  Z  T  G  T  L  E  D  A
L  R  A  F  L  L  C  I  O  A  B  Y  I  R
I  Y  F  L  F  F  A  C  N  P  M  B  E  Y
T  B  F  A  K  E  L  V  Q  P  L  A  N  T
Y  E  R  V  I  F  N  O  E  L  A  S  T  B
C  Z  O  O  Y  E  V  N  W  N  Z  I  D  B
Z  V  N  R  S  H  Y  X  E  E  D  L  C  W
G  A  R  D  E  N  H  U  D  L  R  E  N  J
M  I  N  T  G  A  R  L  I  C  R  S  R  W
```

GARLIC
BASIL
AROMATIC
SAFFRON
QUALITY
CULINARY
DILL
TARRAGON
FLOWER
FENNEL

INGREDIENT
GARDEN
LAVENDER
MARJORAM
MINT
PARSLEY
PLANT
ROSEMARY
FLAVOR
GREEN

91 - Verano

```
T R A V E L M F L G O R M F
V A C A T I O N E S C E E N
G R H V G U Q P I T E L M K
Z H X R B O V K S A A A O D
F A M I L Y Z Q U R C X R I
H C V B O O K S R S C A I V
P J E A A L E A E B Y T E I
Z A O I F F P N G E J I S N
C I T Y S O S D N A B O M G
R U O I Y O E A R C N R N U
M U S I C D T L C H F D U R
Y W W F W M E S Q O T P E R
F R I E N D S J K M R K F N
G A M E S V P J S E E O B H
```

JOY	SEA
FRIENDS	MUSIC
DIVING	TO SWIM
FOOD	LEISURE
STARS	BEACH
FAMILY	MEMORIES
HOME	RELAXATION
GARDEN	SANDALS
GAMES	VACATION
BOOKS	TRAVEL

92 - Insectos

```
F M A Z L M A N T I S B W T
W O R M A O E I G F L E A E
A S N O D T C L R R A E S R
F Q X J Y H O U A N T T P M
O U H C B X C C S P U L B I
D I X K U Q K R S T H E B T
R T C P G D R S H Z O Q U E
A O B Q Q R O H O J R E T Z
G C I C A D A F P D N M T N
O B I A F P C S P X E M E U
N Z E I Y Y H M E N T G R B
F O H E U N E I R B R X F D
L A R V A R E A D S G S L W
Y B M E I W L Z R R N J Y D
```

BEE	LARVA
WASP	DRAGONFLY
HORNET	MANTIS
APHID	BUTTERFLY
CICADA	LADYBUG
COCKROACH	MOSQUITO
BEETLE	MOTH
WORM	FLEA
ANT	GRASSHOPPER
LOCUST	TERMITE

93 - Especias

```
P  F  L  A  V  O  R  N  G  W  C  A  K  T
E  A  N  I  S  E  G  V  A  N  I  L  L  A
P  N  P  B  C  N  W  B  R  O  N  I  O  N
P  S  L  R  B  O  S  A  L  T  N  J  K  W
E  H  Y  Y  I  X  R  R  I  X  A  G  C  M
R  R  R  N  T  K  P  I  C  Q  M  I  L  R
S  O  U  R  T  X  A  G  C  A  O  N  O  E
C  W  N  F  E  N  N  E  L  E  N  G  V  M
U  F  E  H  R  C  U  R  R  Y  N  E  E  A
M  M  Q  E  V  H  L  G  A  D  V  R  B  N
I  X  G  D  T  G  W  Z  S  Z  S  W  W  X
N  U  T  M  E  G  E  Z  T  O  C  Q  K  P
R  T  K  W  D  L  F  I  X  R  H  Q  V  P
A  A  L  G  M  P  S  A  F  F  R  O  N  N
```

SOUR	SWEET
GARLIC	FENNEL
BITTER	GINGER
ANISE	NUTMEG
SAFFRON	PAPRIKA
CINNAMON	PEPPER
ONION	LICORICE
CLOVE	FLAVOR
CUMIN	SALT
CURRY	VANILLA

94 - Emociones

```
P  T  W  X  R  H  S  Y  S  S  B  K  G  G
N  E  R  B  L  I  S  S  A  Y  O  I  R  O
M  R  A  A  N  G  E  R  D  M  R  N  A  Y
I  F  J  C  N  R  I  Q  N  P  E  D  T  M
A  L  O  V  E  Q  Y  H  E  A  D  N  E  G
L  R  Y  T  C  Z  U  D  S  T  O  E  F  K
B  N  A  K  W  M  J  I  S  H  M  S  U  S
S  U  R  P  R  I  S  E  L  Y  X  S  L  M
S  A  T  I  S  F  I  E  D  I  N  T  H  C
K  Z  U  K  W  E  W  C  O  N  T  E  N  T
B  C  H  N  M  A  C  K  L  B  J  Y  N  A
N  E  M  B  A  R  R  A  S  S  E  D  W  E
R  E  L  I  E  F  R  E  L  A  X  E  D  J
O  R  E  T  B  R  Q  L  J  M  X  R  A  S
```

BOREDOM	ANGER
GRATEFUL	FEAR
JOY	PEACE
RELIEF	RELAXED
LOVE	SATISFIED
EMBARRASSED	SYMPATHY
BLISS	SURPRISE
KINDNESS	TRANQUILITY
CALM	SADNESS
CONTENT	

95 - Mediciones

```
T  W  I  D  T  H  S  E  Z  B  Z  M  C  U
O  U  N  C  E  B  C  S  F  W  Q  V  E  Z
N  P  C  T  K  I  L  O  G  R  A  M  N  O
D  M  H  N  W  Q  Y  K  A  D  E  P  T  H
H  E  F  U  E  O  M  I  N  U  T  E  I  I
O  E  C  Y  V  Z  A  L  V  O  L  U  M  E
B  B  I  I  T  C  S  O  I  N  O  D  E  M
W  Y  J  G  M  C  S  M  E  T  E  R  T  Y
L  F  W  M  H  A  D  E  G  R  E  E  E  F
R  I  T  W  L  T  L  T  M  Z  Y  R  R  R
G  D  B  Y  T  E  L  E  N  G  T  H  J  R
W  E  I  G  H  T  G  R  A  M  U  E  Z  F
G  P  L  W  A  Q  Q  J  Y  Y  F  S  N  T
S  M  L  L  N  P  T  H  V  T  E  A  O  Q
```

HEIGHT	LENGTH
WIDTH	MASS
BYTE	METER
CENTIMETER	MINUTE
DECIMAL	OUNCE
DEGREE	WEIGHT
GRAM	DEPTH
KILOGRAM	INCH
KILOMETER	TON
LITER	VOLUME

96 - Barcos

```
W Z U T E K X X S A I L O R
J P Q I Z X A O C E A N F A
P P V D A K J Y G K R R M F
S E A E A B N K A W S L A T
N P C E N G I N E K A A S Z
V M A R I T I M E B I K T C
P J N O E T Y R P U L E E M
L Z O P J W U D U O B U R O
A M E E R I V E R Y O I Y Z
U N F E R R Y G F Q A D M O
D G C Y A C H T A J T I T O
P T S H N A U T I C A L Z F
Q Q E O O R I N P X F L A F
S S U Y X R G Y E Q Q W Z A
```

ANCHOR	SAILOR
RAFT	MARITIME
BUOY	MAST
CANOE	ENGINE
ROPE	NAUTICAL
FERRY	OCEAN
KAYAK	RIVER
LAKE	CREW
SEA	SAILBOAT
TIDE	YACHT

97 - Antártida

```
E M I G R A T I O N S B W H
X T S G E U Y M T W C I A M
P E L L S V C I O J I R T Y
E M A A E T Q N P K E D E G
D P N C A E Y E O B N S R E
I E D I R S C R G T T Y N O
T R S E C P L A R M I S H G
I A M R H E O L A W F Y D R
O T P S E N U S P R I M M A
N U R X R G D G H O C R G P
A R M D P U S I Y C Q A C H
K E N P Q I V E E K E S G Y
C O N T I N E N T Y T C Y O
P E N I N S U L A I C E I J
```

WATER	MIGRATION
BAY	MINERALS
SCIENTIFIC	CLOUDS
CONTINENT	BIRDS
EXPEDITION	PENINSULA
GEOGRAPHY	PENGUINS
GLACIERS	ROCKY
ICE	TEMPERATURE
RESEARCHER	TOPOGRAPHY
ISLANDS	

98 - Piratas

```
B S U J E X Z B D S Q D O C
D H W V O Q H M L A M A P Q
C E F O F E U C C O I N S S
R Z U I R A O P E Y Z G G Q
E Z U E S D C A V E U E H O
W O P Z K L B E A C H R N Q
U N U B S H A N C H O R U I
T P G R Q K D N L S L C E M
C A P T A I N O D C E O R A
T R E A S U R E V A G M C B
K R A D V E N T U R E P W P
X O J E C P M K Q W N A U A
A T X S Y H D F B K D S U Q
D N V J F L A G O L D S A M
```

ANCHOR	PARROT
ADVENTURE	BAD
FLAG	MAP
COMPASS	COINS
CAPTAIN	GOLD
SCAR	DANGER
CAVE	BEACH
SWORD	RUM
ISLAND	TREASURE
LEGEND	CREW

99 - Mamíferos

```
M  D  S  H  E  E  P  D  M  P  W  V  M  K
F  O  X  I  M  W  B  F  J  X  H  M  L  A
O  N  N  Y  C  O  Y  O  T  E  Z  H  O  N
R  K  J  K  Z  L  R  A  B  B  I  T  G  G
O  E  W  E  E  F  G  C  A  T  W  H  O  A
T  Y  E  M  P  Y  E  I  Q  B  Z  O  R  R
C  A  M  E  L  S  W  L  R  Z  F  R  I  O
B  R  N  D  E  H  H  Q  E  A  A  S  L  O
E  Z  W  O  Q  Y  A  V  I  P  F  E  L  Q
A  B  V  L  B  U  L  L  R  L  H  F  A  I
R  V  D  P  G  A  E  D  O  G  P  A  E  V
W  G  M  H  Z  E  B  R  A  O  R  L  N  U
S  Y  K  I  L  N  V  T  I  Z  J  S  Z  T
P  B  O  N  B  K  Q  H  U  F  M  S  C  R
```

WHALE	CAT
DONKEY	GORILLA
HORSE	GIRAFFE
CAMEL	WOLF
KANGAROO	MONKEY
ZEBRA	BEAR
RABBIT	SHEEP
COYOTE	DOG
DOLPHIN	BULL
ELEPHANT	FOX

100 - Abejas

```
P R E C O S Y S T E M H F B
L O T I A W F M G N U O D E
A B L Q T A U R K I W N O N
N V B L H R I Y U C P E X E
T P L G I M I W U I I Y P F
S E O F V N F O O D T A W I
I C S L E L A W I N G S D C
Q X S O L C C T K G W A X I
Z H O W A E H B O A H U V A
U H M E T H N I W R O H D L
H F D R S M O K E D C B P B
A I N S E C T Q U E E N O X
D I V E R S I T Y N E G J X
S U N N Z E S U X F A E J G
```

WINGS	FRUIT
BENEFICIAL	SMOKE
WAX	INSECT
HIVE	GARDEN
FOOD	HONEY
DIVERSITY	PLANTS
ECOSYSTEM	POLLEN
SWARM	POLLINATOR
BLOSSOM	QUEEN
FLOWERS	SUN

1 - Ajedrez

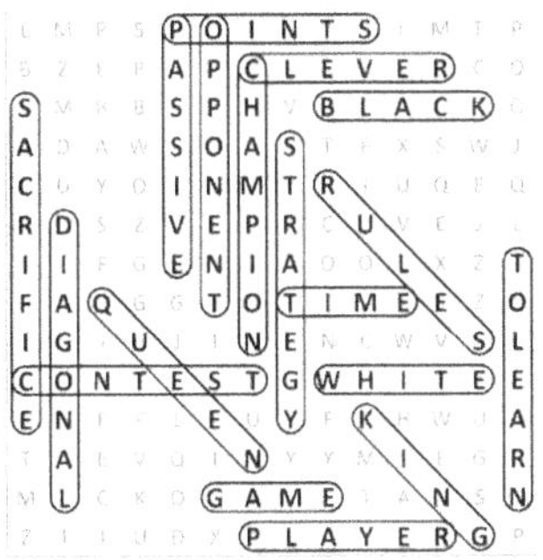

2 - Agua

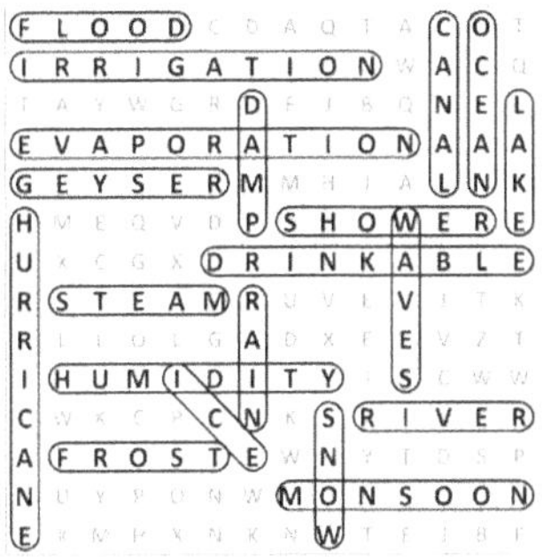

3 - Granja #2

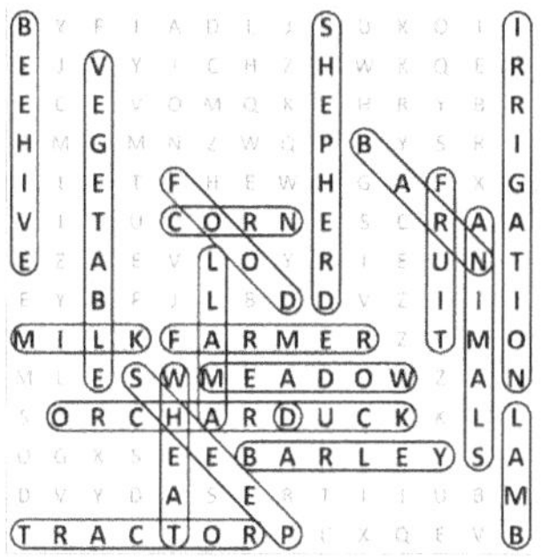

4 - Mueble

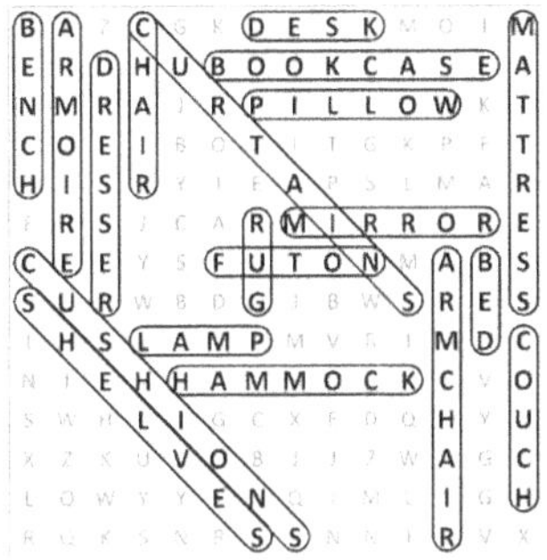

5 - Pesca

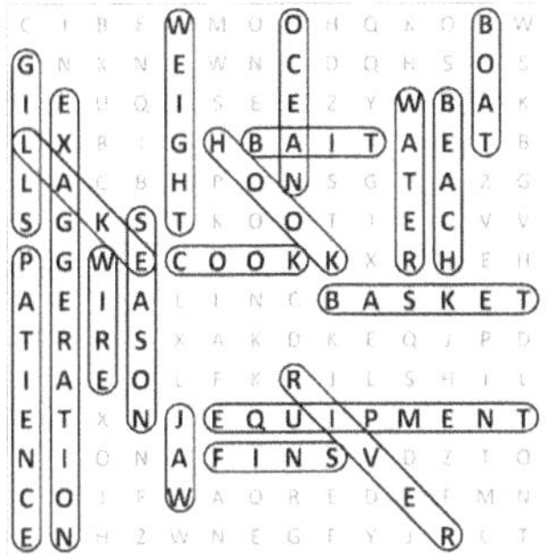

6 - Aviones

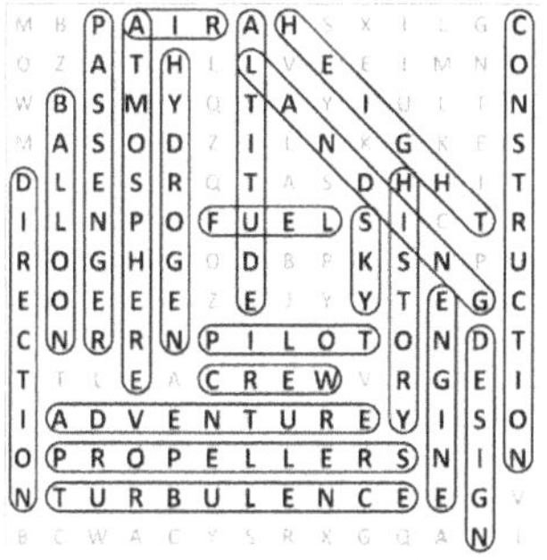

7 - Tipos de Cabello

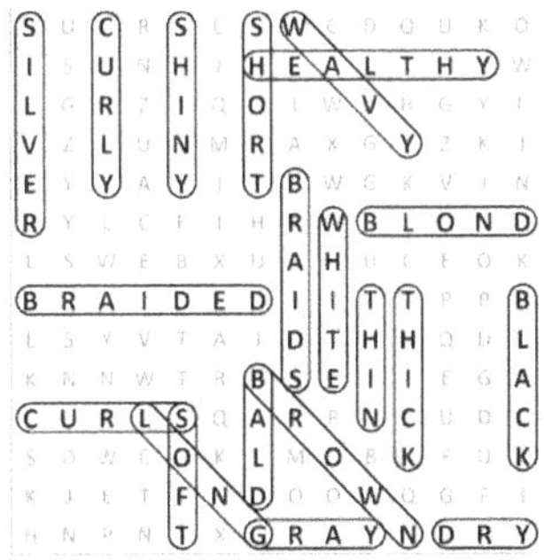

8 - Ciencia Ficción

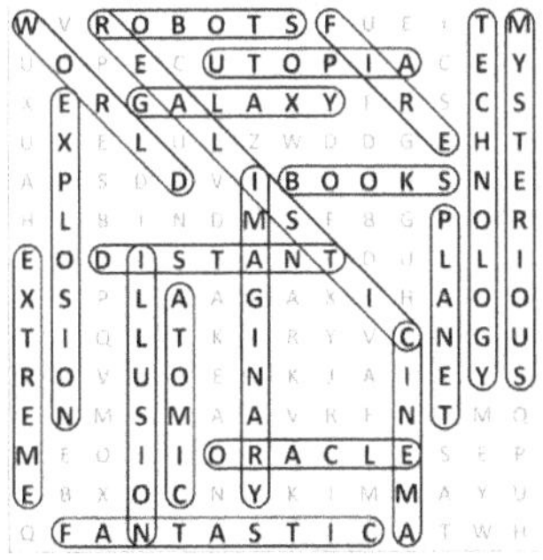

9 - Juguetes

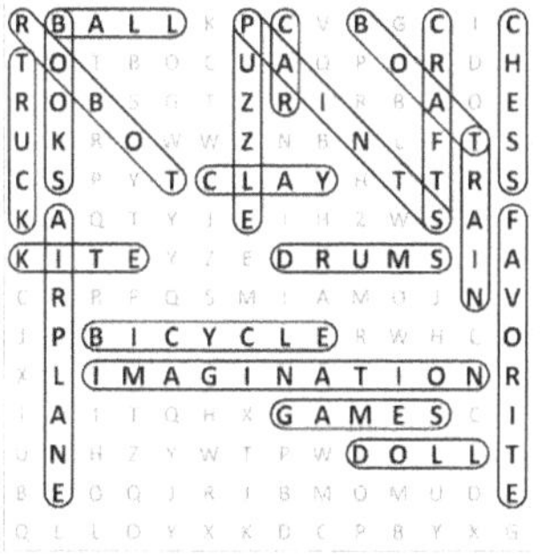

10 - Circo

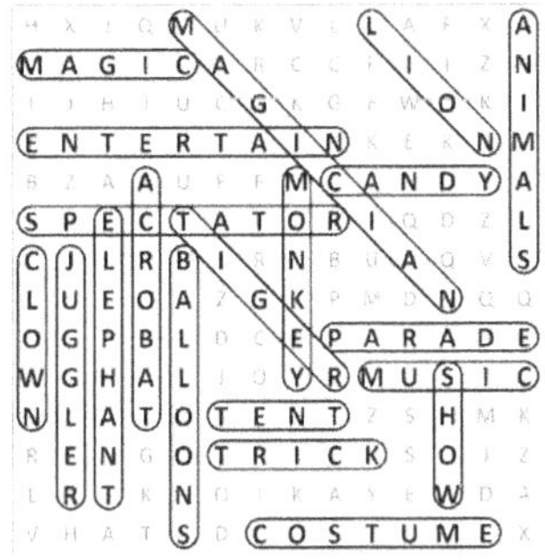

11 - Rellenar

12 - Granja #1

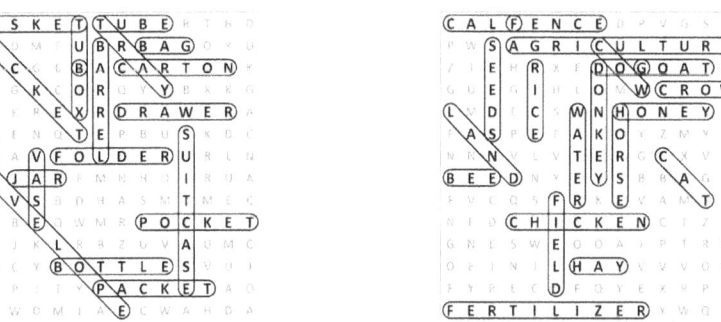

13 - Camping

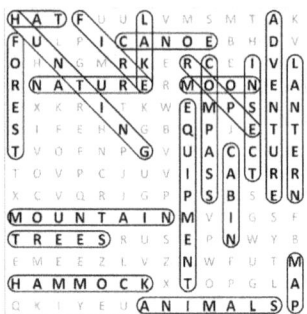

14 - Fruta

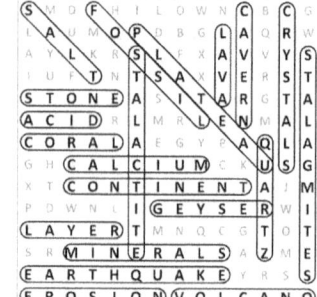

15 - Geología

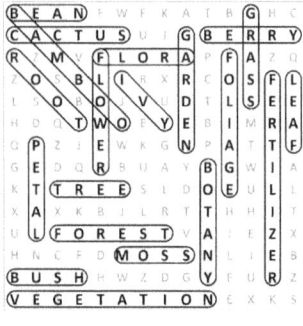

16 - Plantas

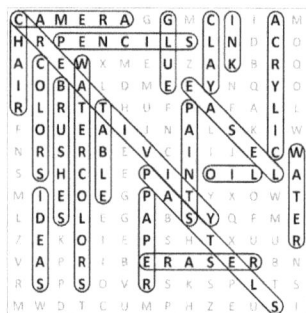

17 - Suministros de Arte

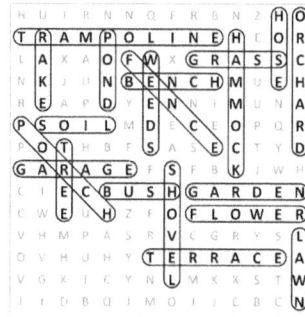

18 - Jardín

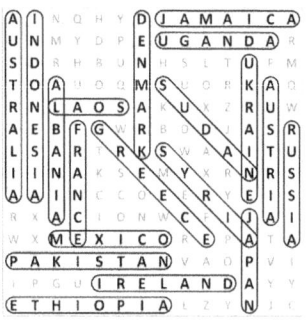

19 - Países #2

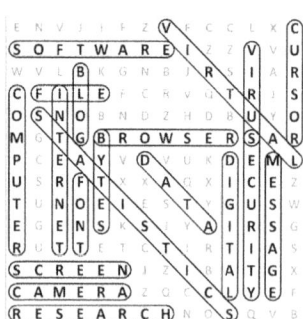

20 - Tecnología

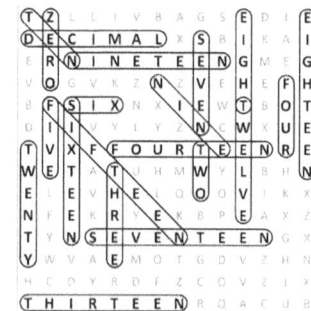

21 - Números

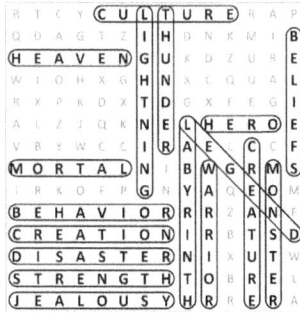

22 - Mitología

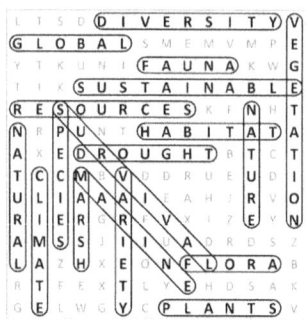

23 - Ecología

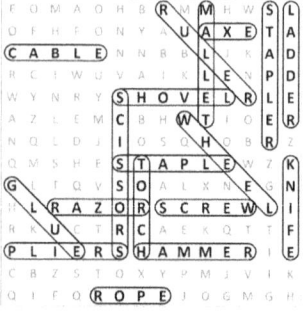

24 - Herramientas

25 - Casa

LIBRARY, FLOOR, DOOR, WALL, ATTIC, FENCE, GARAGE, KIT, SOD, LAMP, FAUCET, BASEMENT, MIRROR, WINDOW

26 - Artes Visuales

MASTERPIECE, VARNISH, CHALK, CLAY, COMPOSITION, CERAMICS, PAINTING, PEN, PENCIL, SCULPTURE, EASEL, FILM, CREATIVITY, PHOTOGRAPH, ARCHITECTURE

27 - Escuela #2

PENCIL, BACKPACK, GAMES, TEACHER, GRAMMAR, COMPUTER, CLOTHE, EDUCATION, LITERATURE, ACADEMIC, DICTIONARY, SUPPLIES, BOOKS, READING, CALENDAR, SCISSORS, LIBRARY

28 - Selva Tropical

MOSS, JUNGLE, BIRDS, DIVERSITY, REFUGE, BOTANICAL, CLOUDS, CLIMATE, AMAZON, HUMIDITY, NEST, RESTORATION, PRESERVATION, INSECT

29 - Colores

YELLOW, RED, PINK, BEIGE, GREEN, BLACK, PURPLE, FUCHSIA, BLUE, MAGENTA, BROWN, VIOLET, GREY

30 - Adjetivos #1

HEAVY, AROMATIC, BRIGHT, DARK, SERIOUS, INNOCENT, SLOW, ATTRACTIVE, IMPORTANT, HONEST, VALUABLE

31 - Familia

GRANDFATHER, DAUGHTER, HUSBAND, BROTHER, ANCESTOR, NIECE, SISTER, WIFE, AUNT, MATERNAL, CHILDREN, NEPHEW, GRANDMOTHER, FATHER, CHILD

32 - Disciplinas Científicas

MINERALOGY, ARCHAEOLOGY, LINGUISTICS, CHEMISTRY, BOTANY, IMMUNOLOGY, BIOLOGY, ECOLOGY, NUTRITION, PSYCHOLOGY, PHYSIOLOGY, BIOCHEMISTRY, ASTRONOMY

33 - Gatos

FUNNY, CLAW, MOUSE, CURIOUS, INDEPENDENT, SLEEP, AFFECTIONATE, PERSONALITY, SHY, PLAYFUL

34 - Cocina

REFRIGERATOR, NAPKIN, FORKS, CUPS, TO EAT, FOOD, JUG, SPONGE, GRILLE, APRON, LADLE

35 - Escuela #1

MAT, MARKERS, LIBRARY, DESK, TO LEARN, CLASSROOM, FRIENDS, PENS, TEACHER, PAPER, CHAIR, ANSWERS, BOOKS, QUIZ

36 - Adjetivos #2

SPICY, CREATIVE, EDIBLE, DRAMATIC, HEALTHY, INTERESTING, NORMAL, SALTY, TIRED, DRY, FAMOUS, DESCRIPTIVE

37 - Cuerpo Humano

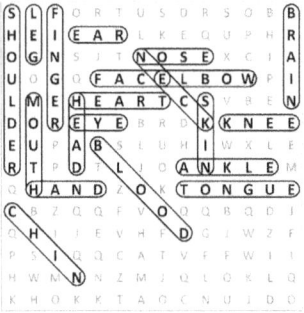

38 - Ciencia

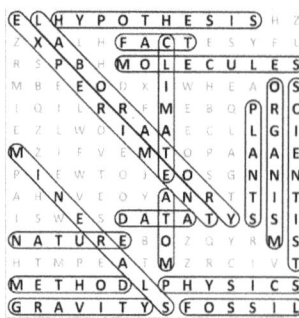

39 - Dinosaurios

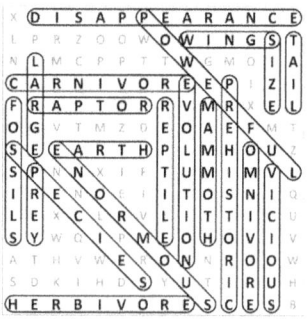

40 - Restaurante #2

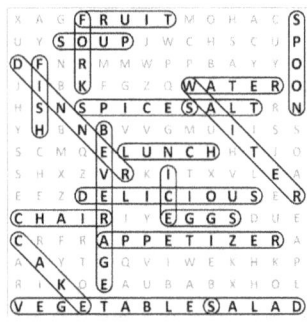

41 - Profesiones #1

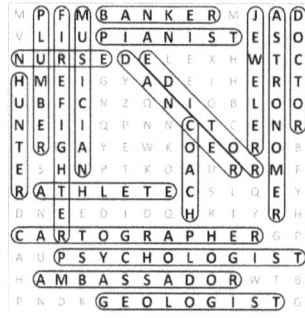

42 - Vehículos

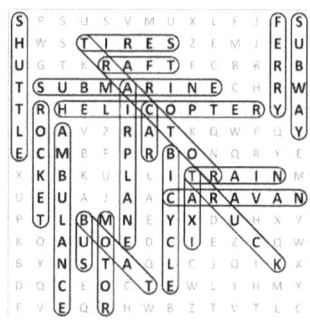

43 - Vacaciones #2

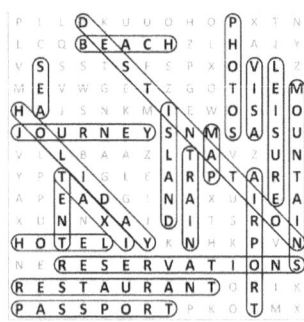

44 - Cumpleaños

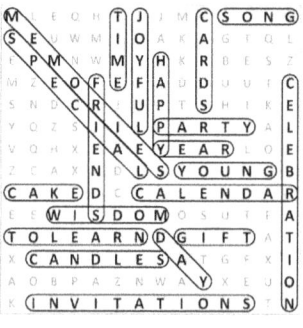

45 - Baile

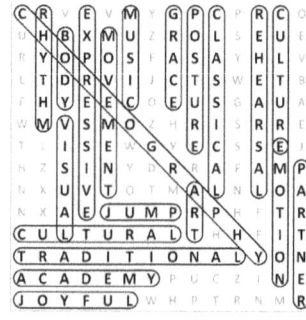

46 - Matemáticas

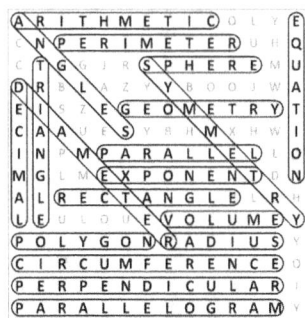

47 - Restaurante #1

48 - Profesiones #2

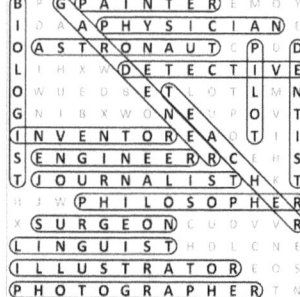

49 - Senderismo

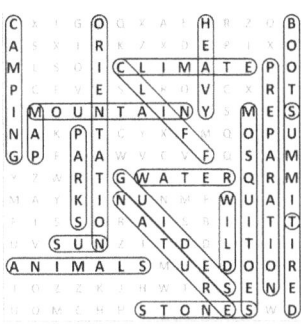

50 - Naturaleza

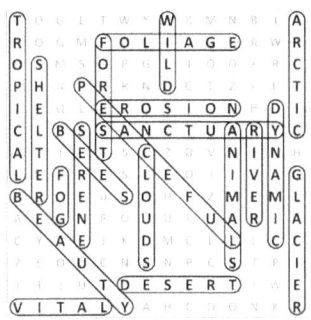

51 - Conduciendo

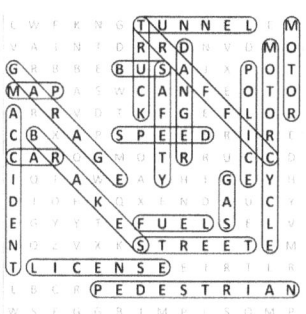

52 - Ballet

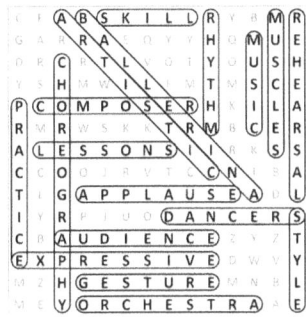

53 - Aventura

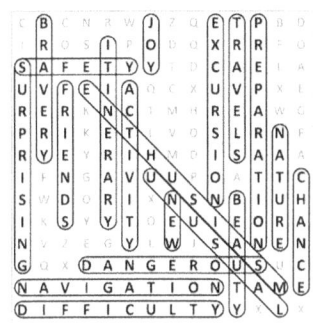

54 - Pájaros

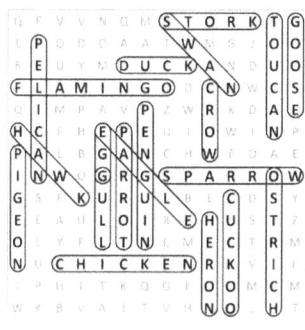

55 - Surf

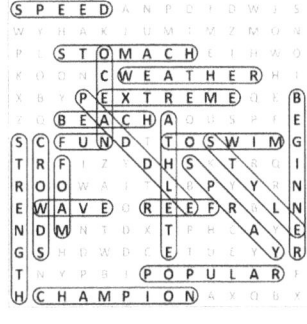

56 - Geografía

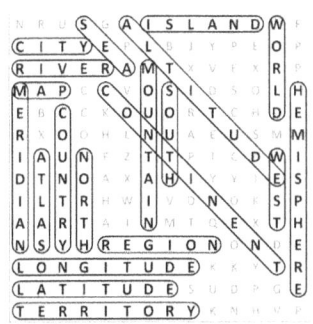

57 - Deportes

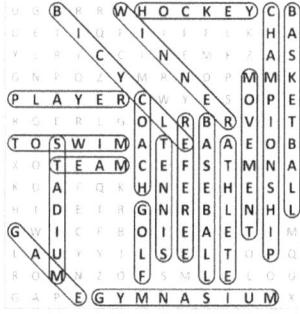

58 - Actividades

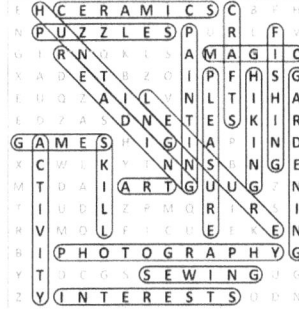

59 - Verduras

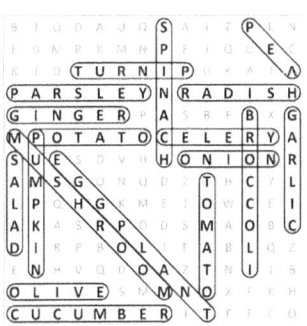

60 - Instrumentos Musicales

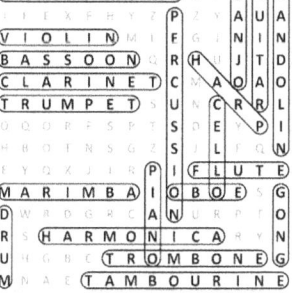

61 - Escalada

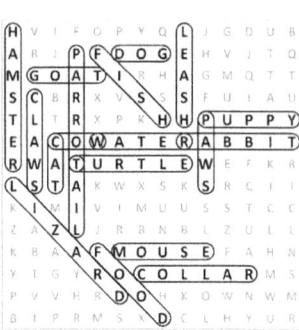

62 - Mascotas

63 - Formas

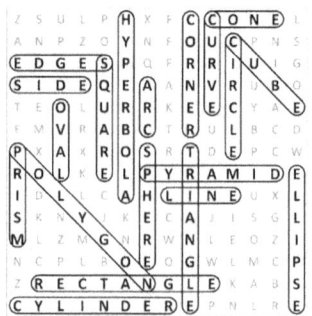

64 - Flores

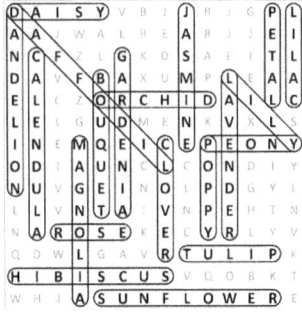

65 - Astronomía

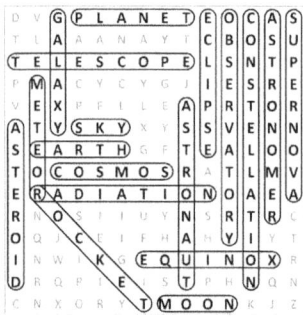

66 - Tiempo

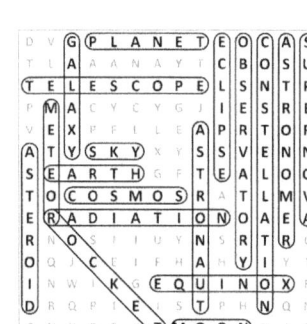

67 - Paisajes

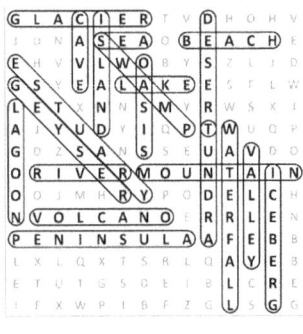

68 - Días y Meses

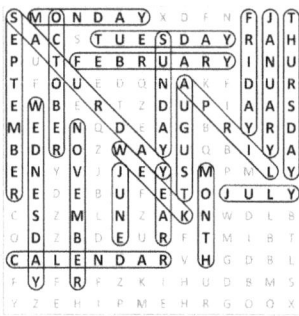

69 - Chocolate

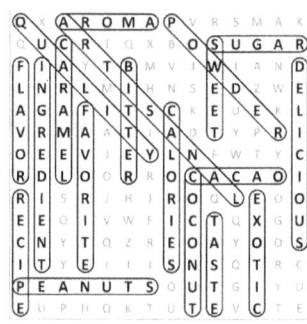

70 - Barbacoas

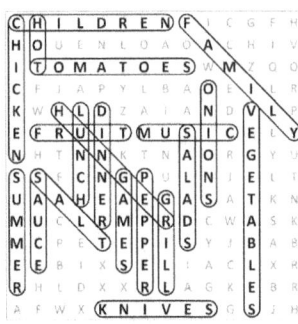

71 - Ropa

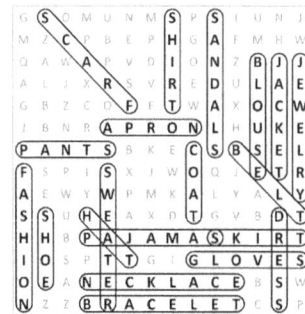

72 - Meditación

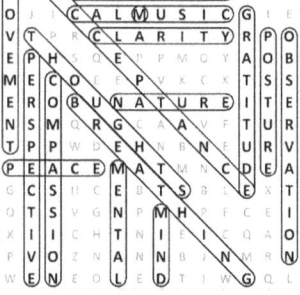

73 - Libros

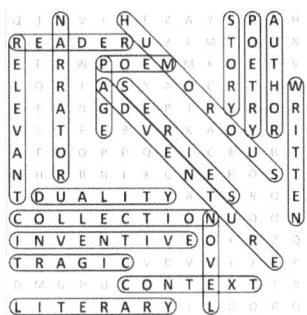

74 - Nutrición

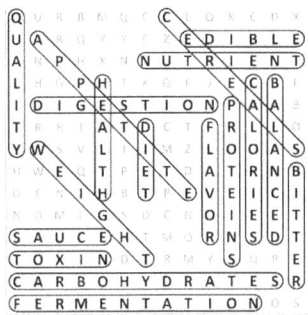

75 - Bondad

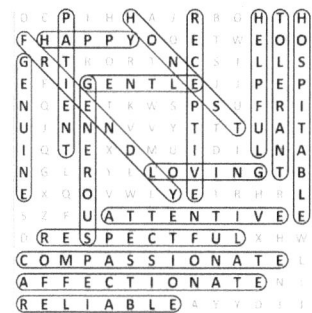

76 - Edificios

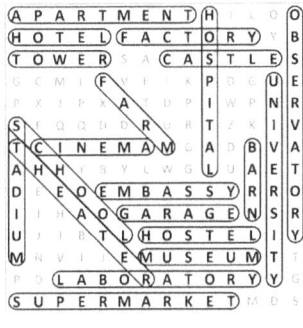

77 - Océano

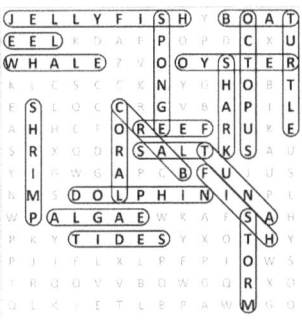

78 - Ciudad

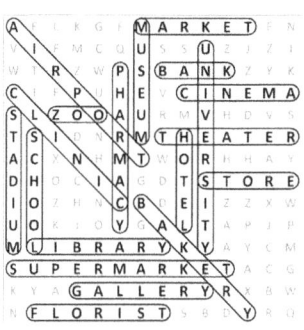

79 - Conservación

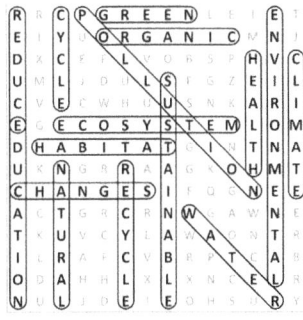

80 - Exploración

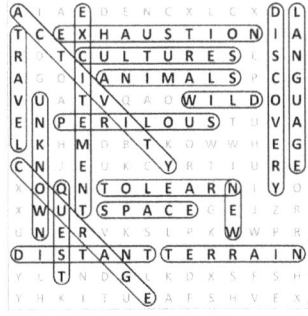

81 - Campeonato

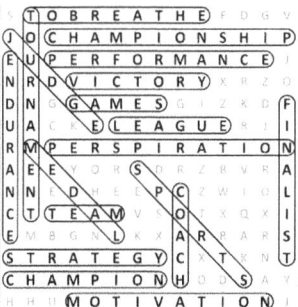

82 - Actividades y Ocio

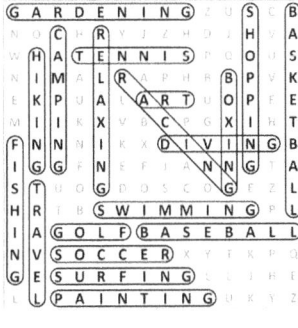

83 - Comida #1

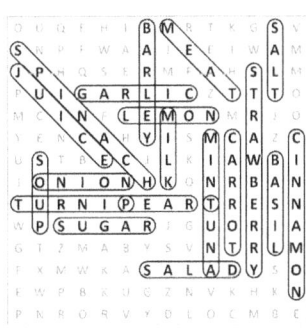

84 - Virtudes #1

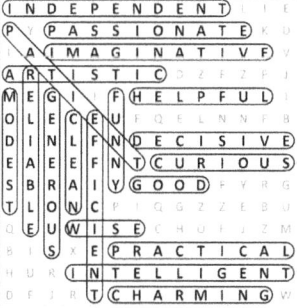

85 - Literatura

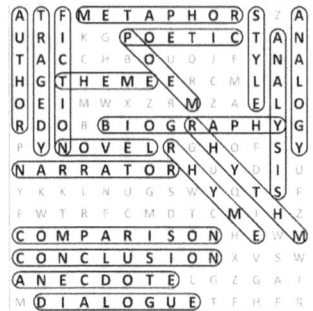

86 - Clima

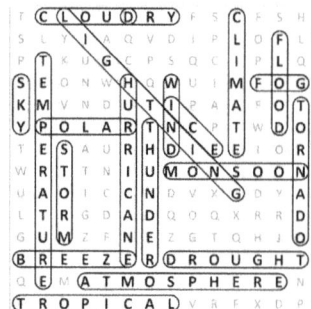

87 - Comida #2

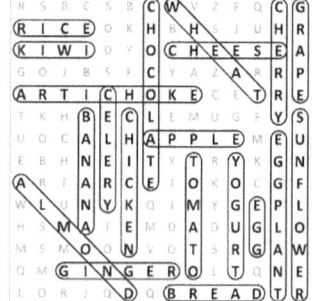

88 - Castillos

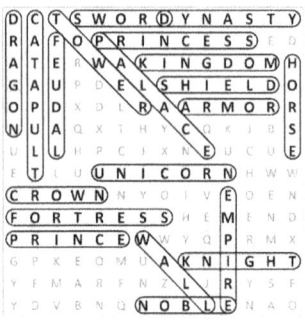

89 - Arte

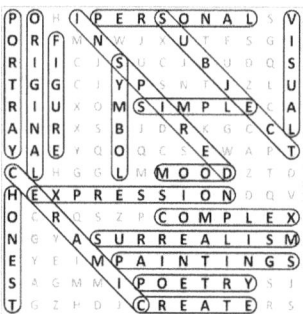

90 - Herboristería

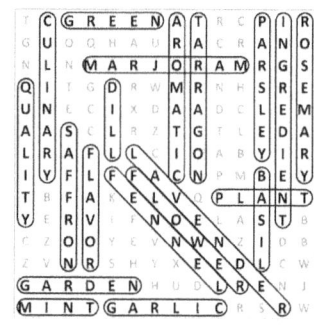

91 - Verano

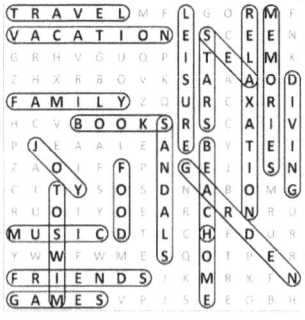

92 - Insectos

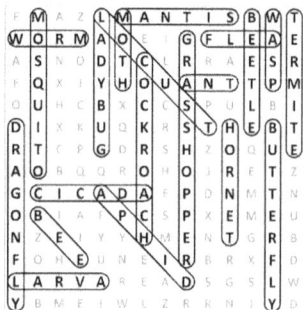

93 - Especias

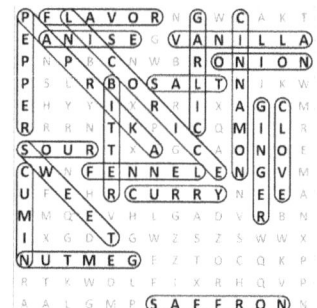

94 - Emociones

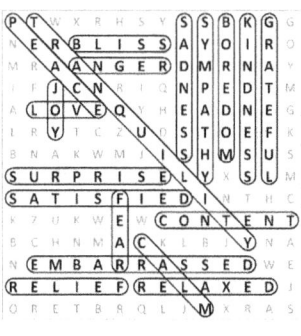

95 - Mediciones

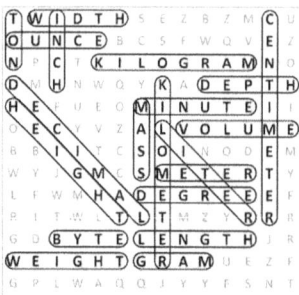

96 - Barcos

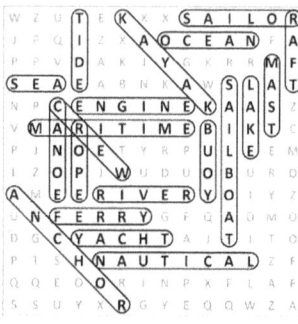

97 - Antártida

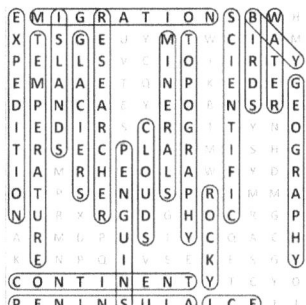

98 - Piratas

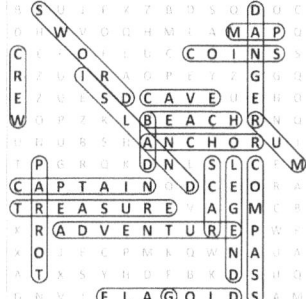

99 - Mamíferos

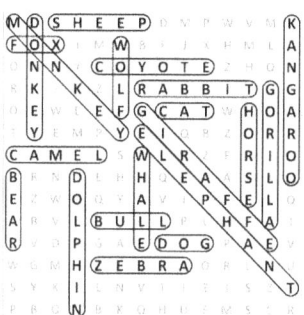

100 - Abejas

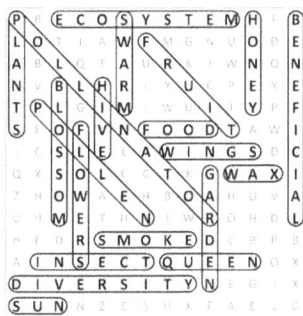

Diccionario

Abejas
Bees

Alas	Wings
Beneficioso	Beneficial
Cera	Wax
Colmena	Hive
Comida	Food
Diversidad	Diversity
Ecosistema	Ecosystem
Enjambre	Swarm
Flor	Blossom
Flores	Flowers
Fruta	Fruit
Humo	Smoke
Insecto	Insect
Jardín	Garden
Miel	Honey
Plantas	Plants
Polen	Pollen
Polinizador	Pollinator
Reina	Queen
Sol	Sun

Actividades
Activities

Actividad	Activity
Arte	Art
Artesanía	Crafts
Caza	Hunting
Cerámica	Ceramics
Costura	Sewing
Fotografía	Photography
Habilidad	Skill
Intereses	Interests
Jardinería	Gardening
Juegos	Games
Lectura	Reading
Magia	Magic
Ocio	Leisure
Pesca	Fishing
Pintura	Painting
Placer	Pleasure
Relajación	Relaxation
Rompecabezas	Puzzles
Senderismo	Hiking

Actividades y Ocio
Activities and Leisure

Arte	Art
Baloncesto	Basketball
Béisbol	Baseball
Boxeo	Boxing
Buceo	Diving
Camping	Camping
Carreras	Racing
Compras	Shopping
Fútbol	Soccer
Golf	Golf
Jardinería	Gardening
Natación	Swimming
Pesca	Fishing
Pintura	Painting
Relajante	Relaxing
Senderismo	Hiking
Surf	Surfing
Tenis	Tennis
Viaje	Travel
Voleibol	Volleyball

Adjetivos #1
Adjectives #1

Absoluto	Absolute
Activo	Active
Ambicioso	Ambitious
Aromático	Aromatic
Atractivo	Attractive
Brillante	Bright
Enorme	Huge
Generoso	Generous
Grande	Large
Honesto	Honest
Importante	Important
Inocente	Innocent
Joven	Young
Lento	Slow
Moderno	Modern
Oscuro	Dark
Perfecto	Perfect
Pesado	Heavy
Serio	Serious
Valioso	Valuable

Adjetivos #2
Adjectives #2

Cansado	Tired
Comestible	Edible
Creativo	Creative
Descriptivo	Descriptive
Dramático	Dramatic
Elegante	Elegant
Famoso	Famous
Fresco	Fresh
Fuerte	Strong
Interesante	Interesting
Natural	Natural
Normal	Normal
Nuevo	New
Orgulloso	Proud
Picante	Spicy
Productivo	Productive
Responsable	Responsible
Salado	Salty
Saludable	Healthy
Seco	Dry

Agua
Water

Canal	Canal
Ducha	Shower
Evaporación	Evaporation
Géiser	Geyser
Helada	Frost
Hielo	Ice
Humedad	Humidity
Huracán	Hurricane
Húmedo	Damp
Inundación	Flood
Lago	Lake
Lluvia	Rain
Monzón	Monsoon
Nieve	Snow
Océano	Ocean
Olas	Waves
Potable	Drinkable
Riego	Irrigation
Río	River
Vapor	Steam

Ajedrez
Chess

Aprender	To Learn
Blanco	White
Campeón	Champion
Concurso	Contest
Diagonal	Diagonal
Estrategia	Strategy
Inteligente	Clever
Juego	Game
Jugador	Player
Negro	Black
Oponente	Opponent
Pasivo	Passive
Puntos	Points
Reglas	Rules
Reina	Queen
Rey	King
Sacrificio	Sacrifice
Tiempo	Time
Torneo	Tournament

Antártida
Antarctica

Agua	Water
Bahía	Bay
Científico	Scientific
Conservación	Conservation
Continente	Continent
Expedición	Expedition
Geografía	Geography
Glaciares	Glaciers
Hielo	Ice
Investigador	Researcher
Islas	Islands
Migración	Migration
Minerales	Minerals
Nubes	Clouds
Pájaros	Birds
Península	Peninsula
Pingüinos	Penguins
Rocoso	Rocky
Temperatura	Temperature
Topografía	Topography

Arte
Art

Cerámica	Ceramic
Complejo	Complex
Composición	Composition
Crear	Create
Escultura	Sculpture
Expresión	Expression
Figura	Figure
Honesto	Honest
Humor	Mood
Inspirado	Inspired
Original	Original
Personal	Personal
Pinturas	Paintings
Poesía	Poetry
Retratar	Portray
Sencillo	Simple
Símbolo	Symbol
Surrealismo	Surrealism
Tema	Subject
Visual	Visual

Artes Visuales
Visual Arts

Arcilla	Clay
Arquitectura	Architecture
Artista	Artist
Barniz	Varnish
Caballete	Easel
Cera	Wax
Cerámica	Ceramics
Composición	Composition
Creatividad	Creativity
Escultura	Sculpture
Fotografía	Photograph
Lápiz	Pencil
Obra Maestra	Masterpiece
Película	Film
Perspectiva	Perspective
Pintura	Painting
Plantilla	Stencil
Pluma	Pen
Retrato	Portrait
Tiza	Chalk

Astronomía
Astronomy

Asteroide	Asteroid
Astronauta	Astronaut
Astrónomo	Astronomer
Cielo	Sky
Cohete	Rocket
Constelación	Constellation
Cosmos	Cosmos
Eclipse	Eclipse
Equinoccio	Equinox
Galaxia	Galaxy
Luna	Moon
Meteoro	Meteor
Observatorio	Observatory
Planeta	Planet
Radiación	Radiation
Satélite	Satellite
Supernova	Supernova
Telescopio	Telescope
Tierra	Earth
Universo	Universe

Aventura
Adventure

Actividad	Activity
Alegría	Joy
Amigos	Friends
Belleza	Beauty
Destino	Destination
Dificultad	Difficulty
Entusiasmo	Enthusiasm
Excursión	Excursion
Inusual	Unusual
Itinerario	Itinerary
Naturaleza	Nature
Navegación	Navigation
Nuevo	New
Oportunidad	Chance
Peligroso	Dangerous
Preparación	Preparation
Seguridad	Safety
Sorprendente	Surprising
Valentía	Bravery
Viajes	Travels

Aviones
Airplanes

Aire	Air
Altitud	Altitude
Altura	Height
Aterrizaje	Landing
Atmósfera	Atmosphere
Aventura	Adventure
Cielo	Sky
Combustible	Fuel
Construcción	Construction
Dirección	Direction
Diseño	Design
Globo	Balloon
Hélices	Propellers
Hidrógeno	Hydrogen
Historia	History
Motor	Engine
Pasajero	Passenger
Piloto	Pilot
Tripulación	Crew
Turbulencia	Turbulence

Baile
Dance

Academia	Academy
Alegre	Joyful
Arte	Art
Clásico	Classical
Coreografía	Choreography
Cuerpo	Body
Cultura	Culture
Cultural	Cultural
Emoción	Emotion
Ensayo	Rehearsal
Expresivo	Expressive
Gracia	Grace
Movimiento	Movement
Música	Music
Postura	Posture
Ritmo	Rhythm
Saltar	Jump
Socio	Partner
Tradicional	Traditional
Visual	Visual

Ballet
Ballet

Aplauso	Applause
Artístico	Artistic
Audiencia	Audience
Bailarina	Ballerina
Bailarines	Dancers
Compositor	Composer
Coreografía	Choreography
Ensayo	Rehearsal
Estilo	Style
Expresivo	Expressive
Gesto	Gesture
Habilidad	Skill
Intensidad	Intensity
Lecciones	Lessons
Músculos	Muscles
Música	Music
Orquesta	Orchestra
Práctica	Practice
Ritmo	Rhythm
Técnica	Technique

Barbacoas
Barbecues

Almuerzo	Lunch
Caliente	Hot
Cebollas	Onions
Cena	Dinner
Cuchillos	Knives
Ensaladas	Salads
Familia	Family
Fruta	Fruit
Hambre	Hunger
Juegos	Games
Música	Music
Niños	Children
Parrilla	Grill
Pimienta	Pepper
Pollo	Chicken
Sal	Salt
Salsa	Sauce
Tomates	Tomatoes
Verano	Summer
Verduras	Vegetables

Barcos
Boats

Ancla	Anchor
Balsa	Raft
Boya	Buoy
Canoa	Canoe
Cuerda	Rope
Ferry	Ferry
Kayak	Kayak
Lago	Lake
Mar	Sea
Marea	Tide
Marinero	Sailor
Marítimo	Maritime
Mástil	Mast
Motor	Engine
Náutico	Nautical
Océano	Ocean
Río	River
Tripulación	Crew
Velero	Sailboat
Yate	Yacht

Bondad
Kindness

Afectuoso	Affectionate
Amistoso	Friendly
Amoroso	Loving
Atento	Attentive
Compasivo	Compassionate
Comprensión	Understanding
Feliz	Happy
Fiable	Reliable
Generoso	Generous
Genuino	Genuine
Honesto	Honest
Hospitalario	Hospitable
Paciente	Patient
Receptivo	Receptive
Respetuoso	Respectful
Suave	Gentle
Tolerante	Tolerant
Útil	Helpful

Campeonato
Championship

Campeonato	Championship
Campeón	Champion
Deportes	Sports
Entrenador	Coach
Equipo	Team
Estrategia	Strategy
Finalista	Finalist
Juegos	Games
Juez	Judge
Liga	League
Medalla	Medal
Motivación	Motivation
Rendimiento	Performance
Resistencia	Endurance
Respirar	To Breathe
Torneo	Tournament
Transpiración	Perspiration
Victoria	Victory

Camping
Camping

Animales	Animals
Aventura	Adventure
Árboles	Trees
Bosque	Forest
Brújula	Compass
Cabina	Cabin
Canoa	Canoe
Caza	Hunting
Cuerda	Rope
Equipo	Equipment
Fuego	Fire
Hamaca	Hammock
Insecto	Insect
Lago	Lake
Linterna	Lantern
Luna	Moon
Mapa	Map
Montaña	Mountain
Naturaleza	Nature
Sombrero	Hat

Casa
House

Alfombra	Rug
Ático	Attic
Biblioteca	Library
Chimenea	Fireplace
Cocina	Kitchen
Dormitorio	Bedroom
Ducha	Shower
Escoba	Broom
Espejo	Mirror
Garaje	Garage
Grifo	Faucet
Jardín	Garden
Lámpara	Lamp
Pared	Wall
Piso	Floor
Puerta	Door
Sótano	Basement
Techo	Roof
Valla	Fence
Ventana	Window

Castillos
Castles

Armadura	Armor
Caballero	Knight
Caballo	Horse
Catapulta	Catapult
Corona	Crown
Dinastía	Dynasty
Dragón	Dragon
Escudo	Shield
Espada	Sword
Feudal	Feudal
Fortaleza	Fortress
Imperio	Empire
Noble	Noble
Palacio	Palace
Pared	Wall
Princesa	Princess
Príncipe	Prince
Reino	Kingdom
Torre	Tower
Unicornio	Unicorn

Chocolate
Chocolate

Amargo	Bitter
Antioxidante	Antioxidant
Aroma	Aroma
Artesanal	Artisanal
Azúcar	Sugar
Cacahuetes	Peanuts
Cacao	Cacao
Calidad	Quality
Calorías	Calories
Caramelo	Caramel
Coco	Coconut
Delicioso	Delicious
Dulce	Sweet
Exótico	Exotic
Favorito	Favorite
Gusto	Taste
Ingrediente	Ingredient
Polvo	Powder
Receta	Recipe
Sabor	Flavor

Ciencia
Science

Átomo	Atom
Científico	Scientist
Clima	Climate
Datos	Data
Evolución	Evolution
Experimento	Experiment
Física	Physics
Fósil	Fossil
Gravedad	Gravity
Hecho	Fact
Hipótesis	Hypothesis
Laboratorio	Laboratory
Método	Method
Minerales	Minerals
Moléculas	Molecules
Naturaleza	Nature
Organismo	Organism
Partículas	Particles
Plantas	Plants
Químico	Chemical

Ciencia Ficción
Science Fiction

Atómico	Atomic
Cine	Cinema
Distante	Distant
Explosión	Explosion
Extremo	Extreme
Fantástico	Fantastic
Fuego	Fire
Futurista	Futuristic
Galaxia	Galaxy
Ilusión	Illusion
Imaginario	Imaginary
Libros	Books
Misterioso	Mysterious
Mundo	World
Oráculo	Oracle
Planeta	Planet
Realista	Realistic
Robots	Robots
Tecnología	Technology
Utopía	Utopia

Circo
Circus

Acróbata	Acrobat
Animales	Animals
Caramelo	Candy
Carpa	Tent
Desfile	Parade
Elefante	Elephant
Entretener	Entertain
Espectador	Spectator
Globos	Balloons
León	Lion
Magia	Magic
Mago	Magician
Malabarista	Juggler
Mono	Monkey
Mostrar	Show
Música	Music
Payaso	Clown
Tigre	Tiger
Traje	Costume
Truco	Trick

Ciudad
Town

Aeropuerto	Airport
Banco	Bank
Biblioteca	Library
Cine	Cinema
Clínica	Clinic
Escuela	School
Estadio	Stadium
Farmacia	Pharmacy
Florista	Florist
Galería	Gallery
Hotel	Hotel
Librería	Bookstore
Mercado	Market
Museo	Museum
Panadería	Bakery
Supermercado	Supermarket
Teatro	Theater
Tienda	Store
Universidad	University
Zoo	Zoo

Clima
Weather

Atmósfera	Atmosphere
Brisa	Breeze
Cielo	Sky
Clima	Climate
Hielo	Ice
Huracán	Hurricane
Inundación	Flood
Monzón	Monsoon
Niebla	Fog
Nube	Cloud
Polar	Polar
Rayo	Lightning
Seco	Dry
Sequía	Drought
Temperatura	Temperature
Tormenta	Storm
Tornado	Tornado
Tropical	Tropical
Trueno	Thunder
Viento	Wind

Cocina
Kitchen

Caldera	Kettle
Comer	To Eat
Comida	Food
Congelador	Freezer
Cucharas	Spoons
Cucharón	Ladle
Cuchillos	Knives
Delantal	Apron
Especias	Spices
Esponja	Sponge
Horno	Oven
Jarra	Jug
Palillos	Chopsticks
Parrilla	Grill
Receta	Recipe
Refrigerador	Refrigerator
Servilleta	Napkin
Tazas	Cups
Tazón	Bowl
Tenedores	Forks

Colores
Colors

Amarillo	Yellow
Azul	Blue
Azur	Azure
Beige	Beige
Blanco	White
Carmesí	Crimson
Cian	Cyan
Fucsia	Fuchsia
Gris	Grey
Índigo	Indigo
Magenta	Magenta
Marrón	Brown
Naranja	Orange
Negro	Black
Púrpura	Purple
Rojo	Red
Rosa	Pink
Sepia	Sepia
Verde	Green
Violeta	Violet

Comida #1
Food #1

Ajo	Garlic
Albahaca	Basil
Atún	Tuna
Azúcar	Sugar
Canela	Cinnamon
Carne	Meat
Cebada	Barley
Cebolla	Onion
Ensalada	Salad
Espinacas	Spinach
Fresa	Strawberry
Jugo	Juice
Leche	Milk
Limón	Lemon
Menta	Mint
Nabo	Turnip
Pera	Pear
Sal	Salt
Sopa	Soup
Zanahoria	Carrot

Comida #2
Food #2

Alcachofa	Artichoke
Almendra	Almond
Apio	Celery
Arroz	Rice
Berenjena	Eggplant
Cereza	Cherry
Chocolate	Chocolate
Girasol	Sunflower
Huevo	Egg
Jengibre	Ginger
Kiwi	Kiwi
Manzana	Apple
Pan	Bread
Plátano	Banana
Pollo	Chicken
Queso	Cheese
Tomate	Tomato
Trigo	Wheat
Uva	Grape
Yogur	Yogurt

Conduciendo
Driving

Accidente	Accident
Autobús	Bus
Calle	Street
Camión	Truck
Coche	Car
Combustible	Fuel
Frenos	Brakes
Garaje	Garage
Gas	Gas
Licencia	License
Mapa	Map
Motocicleta	Motorcycle
Motor	Motor
Peatonal	Pedestrian
Peligro	Danger
Policía	Police
Seguridad	Safety
Tráfico	Traffic
Túnel	Tunnel
Velocidad	Speed

Conservación
Conservation

Agua	Water
Ambiental	Environmental
Cambios	Changes
Ciclo	Cycle
Clima	Climate
Contaminación	Pollution
Ecosistema	Ecosystem
Educación	Education
Hábitat	Habitat
Natural	Natural
Orgánico	Organic
Pesticida	Pesticide
Preocupación	Concern
Reciclar	Recycle
Reducir	Reduce
Salud	Health
Sostenible	Sustainable
Verde	Green
Voluntario	Volunteer

Cuerpo Humano
Human Body

Barbilla	Chin
Boca	Mouth
Cabeza	Head
Cara	Face
Cerebro	Brain
Codo	Elbow
Corazón	Heart
Cuello	Neck
Dedo	Finger
Hombro	Shoulder
Lengua	Tongue
Mano	Hand
Nariz	Nose
Ojo	Eye
Oreja	Ear
Piel	Skin
Pierna	Leg
Rodilla	Knee
Sangre	Blood
Tobillo	Ankle

Cumpleaños
Birthday

Alegre	Joyful
Amigos	Friends
Año	Year
Aprender	To Learn
Calendario	Calendar
Canción	Song
Celebración	Celebration
Día	Day
Especial	Special
Feliz	Happy
Invitaciones	Invitations
Joven	Young
Partido	Party
Pastel	Cake
Recuerdos	Memories
Regalo	Gift
Sabiduría	Wisdom
Tarjetas	Cards
Tiempo	Time
Velas	Candles

Deportes
Sports

Atleta	Athlete
Árbitro	Referee
Baloncesto	Basketball
Béisbol	Baseball
Bicicleta	Bicycle
Campeonato	Championship
Entrenador	Coach
Equipo	Team
Estadio	Stadium
Ganador	Winner
Gimnasia	Gymnastics
Gimnasio	Gymnasium
Golf	Golf
Hockey	Hockey
Juego	Game
Jugador	Player
Movimiento	Movement
Nadar	To Swim
Tenis	Tennis

Dinosaurios
Dinosaurs

Alas	Wings
Carnívoro	Carnivore
Cola	Tail
Desaparición	Disappearance
Enorme	Enormous
Especie	Species
Evolución	Evolution
Fósiles	Fossils
Grande	Large
Herbívoro	Herbivore
Mamut	Mammoth
Omnívoro	Omnivore
Poderoso	Powerful
Prehistórico	Prehistoric
Presa	Prey
Raptor	Raptor
Reptil	Reptile
Tamaño	Size
Tierra	Earth
Vicioso	Vicious

Disciplinas Científicas
Scientific Disciplines

Anatomía	Anatomy
Arqueología	Archaeology
Astronomía	Astronomy
Biología	Biology
Bioquímica	Biochemistry
Botánica	Botany
Ecología	Ecology
Fisiología	Physiology
Geología	Geology
Inmunología	Immunology
Lingüística	Linguistics
Mecánica	Mechanics
Meteorología	Meteorology
Mineralogía	Mineralogy
Neurología	Neurology
Nutrición	Nutrition
Psicología	Psychology
Química	Chemistry
Sociología	Sociology
Zoología	Zoology

Días y Meses
Days and Months

Abril	April
Agosto	August
Año	Year
Calendario	Calendar
Domingo	Sunday
Enero	January
Febrero	February
Jueves	Thursday
Julio	July
Junio	June
Lunes	Monday
Martes	Tuesday
Mes	Month
Miércoles	Wednesday
Noviembre	November
Octubre	October
Sábado	Saturday
Semana	Week
Septiembre	September
Viernes	Friday

Ecología
Ecology

Clima	Climate
Comunidades	Communities
Diversidad	Diversity
Especie	Species
Fauna	Fauna
Flora	Flora
Global	Global
Hábitat	Habitat
Marino	Marine
Natural	Natural
Naturaleza	Nature
Pantano	Marsh
Plantas	Plants
Recursos	Resources
Sequía	Drought
Sostenible	Sustainable
Supervivencia	Survival
Variedad	Variety
Vegetación	Vegetation
Voluntarios	Volunteers

Edificios
Buildings

Albergue	Hostel
Apartamento	Apartment
Castillo	Castle
Cine	Cinema
Embajada	Embassy
Escuela	School
Estadio	Stadium
Fábrica	Factory
Garaje	Garage
Granero	Barn
Granja	Farm
Hospital	Hospital
Hotel	Hotel
Laboratorio	Laboratory
Museo	Museum
Observatorio	Observatory
Supermercado	Supermarket
Teatro	Theater
Torre	Tower
Universidad	University

Emociones
Emotions

Aburrimiento	Boredom
Agradecido	Grateful
Alegría	Joy
Alivio	Relief
Amor	Love
Avergonzado	Embarrassed
Beatitud	Bliss
Bondad	Kindness
Calma	Calm
Contenido	Content
Ira	Anger
Miedo	Fear
Paz	Peace
Relajado	Relaxed
Satisfecho	Satisfied
Simpatía	Sympathy
Sorpresa	Surprise
Ternura	Tenderness
Tranquilidad	Tranquility
Tristeza	Sadness

Escalada
Climbing

Altitud	Altitude
Atmósfera	Atmosphere
Botas	Boots
Casco	Helmet
Cueva	Cave
Curiosidad	Curiosity
Estabilidad	Stability
Estrecho	Narrow
Experto	Expert
Físico	Physical
Formación	Training
Fuerza	Strength
Guantes	Gloves
Guías	Guides
Lesión	Injury
Mapa	Map
Senderismo	Hiking
Terreno	Terrain

Escuela #1
School #1

Alfabeto	Alphabet
Almuerzo	Lunch
Amigos	Friends
Aprender	To Learn
Aula	Classroom
Biblioteca	Library
Carpetas	Folders
Escritorio	Desk
Examen	Quiz
Exámenes	Exams
Lápiz	Pencil
Libros	Books
Marcadores	Markers
Matemática	Math
Números	Numbers
Papel	Paper
Plumas	Pens
Profesor	Teacher
Respuestas	Answers
Silla	Chair

Escuela #2
School #2

Académico	Academic
Autobús	Bus
Biblioteca	Library
Calendario	Calendar
Ciencia	Science
Diccionario	Dictionary
Educación	Education
Gramática	Grammar
Juegos	Games
Lápiz	Pencil
Lectura	Reading
Libros	Books
Literatura	Literature
Mochila	Backpack
Ordenador	Computer
Papel	Paper
Profesor	Teacher
Ropa	Clothes
Suministros	Supplies
Tijeras	Scissors

Especias
Spices

Agrio	Sour
Ajo	Garlic
Amargo	Bitter
Anís	Anise
Azafrán	Saffron
Canela	Cinnamon
Cebolla	Onion
Clavo	Clove
Comino	Cumin
Curry	Curry
Dulce	Sweet
Hinojo	Fennel
Jengibre	Ginger
Nuez Moscada	Nutmeg
Pimentón	Paprika
Pimienta	Pepper
Regaliz	Licorice
Sabor	Flavor
Sal	Salt
Vainilla	Vanilla

Exploración
Exploration

Actividad	Activity
Agotamiento	Exhaustion
Animales	Animals
Aprender	To Learn
Búsqueda	Quest
Coraje	Courage
Culturas	Cultures
Desconocido	Unknown
Descubrimiento	Discovery
Determinación	Determination
Distante	Distant
Emoción	Excitement
Espacio	Space
Idioma	Language
Nuevo	New
Peligroso	Perilous
Salvaje	Wild
Terreno	Terrain
Viaje	Travel

Familia
Family

Abuela	Grandmother
Abuelo	Grandfather
Antepasado	Ancestor
Esposa	Wife
Hermana	Sister
Hermano	Brother
Hija	Daughter
Infancia	Childhood
Madre	Mother
Marido	Husband
Materno	Maternal
Nieto	Grandson
Niño	Child
Niños	Children
Padre	Father
Primo	Cousin
Sobrina	Niece
Sobrino	Nephew
Tía	Aunt
Tío	Uncle

Flores
Flowers

Amapola	Poppy
Caléndula	Calendula
Diente de León	Dandelion
Gardenia	Gardenia
Girasol	Sunflower
Hibisco	Hibiscus
Jazmín	Jasmine
Lavanda	Lavender
Lila	Lilac
Lirio	Lily
Magnolia	Magnolia
Margarita	Daisy
Narciso	Daffodil
Orquídea	Orchid
Peonía	Peony
Pétalo	Petal
Ramo	Bouquet
Rosa	Rose
Trébol	Clover
Tulipán	Tulip

Formas
Shapes

Arco	Arc
Bordes	Edges
Cilindro	Cylinder
Círculo	Circle
Cono	Cone
Cuadrado	Square
Cubo	Cube
Curva	Curve
Elipse	Ellipse
Esfera	Sphere
Esquina	Corner
Hipérbola	Hyperbola
Lado	Side
Línea	Line
Oval	Oval
Pirámide	Pyramid
Polígono	Polygon
Prisma	Prism
Rectángulo	Rectangle
Triángulo	Triangle

Fruta
Fruit

Aguacate	Avocado
Albaricoque	Apricot
Baya	Berry
Cereza	Cherry
Coco	Coconut
Frambuesa	Raspberry
Guayaba	Guava
Kiwi	Kiwi
Limón	Lemon
Mango	Mango
Manzana	Apple
Melocotón	Peach
Melón	Melon
Naranja	Orange
Nectarina	Nectarine
Papaya	Papaya
Pera	Pear
Piña	Pineapple
Plátano	Banana
Uva	Grape

Gatos
Cats

Afectuoso	Affectionate
Cazador	Hunter
Cola	Tail
Curioso	Curious
Dormir	Sleep
Garra	Claw
Gracioso	Funny
Hilo	Yarn
Independiente	Independent
Juguetón	Playful
Loco	Crazy
Pata	Paw
Personalidad	Personality
Piel	Fur
Poco	Little
Ratón	Mouse
Rápido	Fast
Salvaje	Wild
Tímido	Shy

Geografía
Geography

Altitud	Altitude
Atlas	Atlas
Ciudad	City
Continente	Continent
Hemisferio	Hemisphere
Isla	Island
Latitud	Latitude
Longitud	Longitude
Mapa	Map
Mar	Sea
Meridiano	Meridian
Montaña	Mountain
Mundo	World
Norte	North
Oeste	West
País	Country
Región	Region
Río	River
Sur	South
Territorio	Territory

Geología
Geology

Ácido	Acid
Calcio	Calcium
Capa	Layer
Caverna	Cavern
Continente	Continent
Coral	Coral
Cristales	Crystals
Cuarzo	Quartz
Erosión	Erosion
Estalactita	Stalactite
Estalagmitas	Stalagmites
Fósil	Fossil
Géiser	Geyser
Lava	Lava
Meseta	Plateau
Minerales	Minerals
Piedra	Stone
Sal	Salt
Terremoto	Earthquake
Volcán	Volcano

Granja #1
Farm #1

Abeja	Bee
Agricultura	Agriculture
Agua	Water
Arroz	Rice
Burro	Donkey
Caballo	Horse
Cabra	Goat
Campo	Field
Cuervo	Crow
Fertilizante	Fertilizer
Gato	Cat
Heno	Hay
Miel	Honey
Perro	Dog
Pollo	Chicken
Semillas	Seeds
Ternero	Calf
Tierra	Land
Vaca	Cow
Valla	Fence

Granja #2
Farm #2

Agricultor	Farmer
Animales	Animals
Cebada	Barley
Colmena	Beehive
Comida	Food
Cordero	Lamb
Fruta	Fruit
Granero	Barn
Huerto	Orchard
Leche	Milk
Llama	Llama
Maíz	Corn
Oveja	Sheep
Pastor	Shepherd
Pato	Duck
Prado	Meadow
Riego	Irrigation
Tractor	Tractor
Trigo	Wheat
Vegetal	Vegetable

Herboristería
Herbalism

Ajo	Garlic
Albahaca	Basil
Aromático	Aromatic
Azafrán	Saffron
Calidad	Quality
Culinario	Culinary
Eneldo	Dill
Estragón	Tarragon
Flor	Flower
Hinojo	Fennel
Ingrediente	Ingredient
Jardín	Garden
Lavanda	Lavender
Mejorana	Marjoram
Menta	Mint
Perejil	Parsley
Planta	Plant
Romero	Rosemary
Sabor	Flavor
Verde	Green

Herramientas
Tools

Alicates	Pliers
Antorcha	Torch
Cable	Cable
Cuchillo	Knife
Cuerda	Rope
Escalera	Ladder
Grapa	Staple
Grapadora	Stapler
Hacha	Axe
Martillo	Hammer
Mazo	Mallet
Navaja	Razor
Pala	Shovel
Pegamento	Glue
Regla	Ruler
Rueda	Wheel
Tijeras	Scissors
Tornillo	Screw

Insectos
Insects

Abeja	Bee
Avispa	Wasp
Avispón	Hornet
Áfido	Aphid
Cigarra	Cicada
Cucaracha	Cockroach
Escarabajo	Beetle
Gusano	Worm
Hormiga	Ant
Langosta	Locust
Larva	Larva
Libélula	Dragonfly
Mantis	Mantis
Mariposa	Butterfly
Mariquita	Ladybug
Mosquito	Mosquito
Polilla	Moth
Pulga	Flea
Saltamontes	Grasshopper
Termita	Termite

Instrumentos Musicales
Musical Instruments

Armónica	Harmonica
Arpa	Harp
Banjo	Banjo
Clarinete	Clarinet
Fagot	Bassoon
Flauta	Flute
Gong	Gong
Guitarra	Guitar
Mandolina	Mandolin
Marimba	Marimba
Oboe	Oboe
Pandereta	Tambourine
Percusión	Percussion
Piano	Piano
Saxofón	Saxophone
Tambor	Drum
Trombón	Trombone
Trompeta	Trumpet
Violín	Violin
Violonchelo	Cello

Jardín
Garden

Arbusto	Bush
Árbol	Tree
Banco	Bench
Césped	Lawn
Estanque	Pond
Flor	Flower
Garaje	Garage
Hamaca	Hammock
Hierba	Grass
Huerto	Orchard
Jardín	Garden
Malezas	Weeds
Manguera	Hose
Pala	Shovel
Porche	Porch
Rastrillo	Rake
Suelo	Soil
Terraza	Terrace
Trampolín	Trampoline
Valla	Fence

Juguetes
Toys

Ajedrez	Chess
Arcilla	Clay
Artesanía	Crafts
Avión	Airplane
Barco	Boat
Bicicleta	Bicycle
Bola	Ball
Camión	Truck
Coche	Car
Cometa	Kite
Favorito	Favorite
Imaginación	Imagination
Juegos	Games
Libros	Books
Muñeca	Doll
Pinturas	Paints
Robot	Robot
Rompecabezas	Puzzle
Tambores	Drums
Tren	Train

Libros
Books

Autor	Author
Aventura	Adventure
Colección	Collection
Contexto	Context
Dualidad	Duality
Escrito	Written
Historia	Story
Histórico	Historical
Humorístico	Humorous
Inventivo	Inventive
Lector	Reader
Literario	Literary
Narrador	Narrator
Novela	Novel
Página	Page
Pertinente	Relevant
Poema	Poem
Poesía	Poetry
Serie	Series
Trágico	Tragic

Literatura
Literature

Analogía	Analogy
Análisis	Analysis
Anécdota	Anecdote
Autor	Author
Biografía	Biography
Comparación	Comparison
Conclusión	Conclusion
Descripción	Description
Diálogo	Dialogue
Estilo	Style
Ficción	Fiction
Metáfora	Metaphor
Narrador	Narrator
Novela	Novel
Poema	Poem
Poético	Poetic
Rima	Rhyme
Ritmo	Rhythm
Tema	Theme
Tragedia	Tragedy

Mamíferos
Mammals

Ballena	Whale
Burro	Donkey
Caballo	Horse
Camello	Camel
Canguro	Kangaroo
Cebra	Zebra
Conejo	Rabbit
Coyote	Coyote
Delfín	Dolphin
Elefante	Elephant
Gato	Cat
Gorila	Gorilla
Jirafa	Giraffe
Lobo	Wolf
Mono	Monkey
Oso	Bear
Oveja	Sheep
Perro	Dog
Toro	Bull
Zorro	Fox

Mascotas
Pets

Agua	Water
Cabra	Goat
Cachorro	Puppy
Cola	Tail
Collar	Collar
Comida	Food
Conejo	Rabbit
Correa	Leash
Garras	Claws
Gato	Cat
Hámster	Hamster
Lagarto	Lizard
Loro	Parrot
Patas	Paws
Perro	Dog
Pescado	Fish
Ratón	Mouse
Tortuga	Turtle
Vaca	Cow
Veterinario	Veterinarian

Matemáticas
Math

Aritmética	Arithmetic
Ángulos	Angles
Circunferencia	Circumference
Decimal	Decimal
Diámetro	Diameter
Ecuación	Equation
Esfera	Sphere
Exponente	Exponent
Fracción	Fraction
Geometría	Geometry
Paralelo	Parallel
Paralelogramo	Parallelogram
Perímetro	Perimeter
Perpendicular	Perpendicular
Polígono	Polygon
Radio	Radius
Rectángulo	Rectangle
Simetría	Symmetry
Triángulo	Triangle
Volumen	Volume

Mediciones
Measurements

Altura	Height
Ancho	Width
Byte	Byte
Centímetro	Centimeter
Decimal	Decimal
Grado	Degree
Gramo	Gram
Kilogramo	Kilogram
Kilómetro	Kilometer
Litro	Liter
Longitud	Length
Masa	Mass
Metro	Meter
Minuto	Minute
Onza	Ounce
Peso	Weight
Profundidad	Depth
Pulgada	Inch
Tonelada	Ton
Volumen	Volume

Meditación
Meditation

Aceptación	Acceptance
Atención	Attention
Bondad	Kindness
Calma	Calm
Claridad	Clarity
Compasión	Compassion
Emociones	Emotions
Gratitud	Gratitude
Mental	Mental
Mente	Mind
Movimiento	Movement
Música	Music
Naturaleza	Nature
Observación	Observation
Paz	Peace
Pensamientos	Thoughts
Perspectiva	Perspective
Postura	Posture
Respiración	Breathing
Silencio	Silence

Mitología
Mythology

Arquetipo	Archetype
Celos	Jealousy
Cielo	Heaven
Comportamiento	Behavior
Creación	Creation
Creencias	Beliefs
Criatura	Creature
Cultura	Culture
Desastre	Disaster
Fuerza	Strength
Guerrero	Warrior
Héroe	Hero
Inmortalidad	Immortality
Laberinto	Labyrinth
Leyenda	Legend
Monstruo	Monster
Mortal	Mortal
Rayo	Lightning
Trueno	Thunder
Venganza	Revenge

Mueble
Furniture

Alfombra	Rug
Almohada	Pillow
Armario	Armoire
Banco	Bench
Cama	Bed
Cojines	Cushions
Colchón	Mattress
Cortinas	Curtains
Cómoda	Dresser
Edredones	Comforters
Escritorio	Desk
Espejo	Mirror
Estantería	Bookcase
Estantes	Shelves
Futón	Futon
Hamaca	Hammock
Lámpara	Lamp
Silla	Chair
Sillón	Armchair
Sofá	Couch

Naturaleza
Nature

Abejas	Bees
Animales	Animals
Ártico	Arctic
Belleza	Beauty
Bosque	Forest
Desierto	Desert
Dinámico	Dynamic
Erosión	Erosion
Follaje	Foliage
Glaciar	Glacier
Niebla	Fog
Nubes	Clouds
Pacífico	Peaceful
Refugio	Shelter
Río	River
Salvaje	Wild
Santuario	Sanctuary
Sereno	Serene
Tropical	Tropical
Vital	Vital

Nutrición
Nutrition

Amargo	Bitter
Apetito	Appetite
Calidad	Quality
Calorías	Calories
Carbohidratos	Carbohydrates
Cereales	Cereals
Comestible	Edible
Dieta	Diet
Digestión	Digestion
Equilibrado	Balanced
Fermentación	Fermentation
Nutriente	Nutrient
Peso	Weight
Proteínas	Proteins
Sabor	Flavor
Salsa	Sauce
Salud	Health
Saludable	Healthy
Toxina	Toxin
Vitamina	Vitamin

Números
Numbers

Catorce	Fourteen
Cero	Zero
Cinco	Five
Cuatro	Four
Decimal	Decimal
Diecinueve	Nineteen
Dieciocho	Eighteen
Dieciséis	Sixteen
Diecisiete	Seventeen
Diez	Ten
Doce	Twelve
Dos	Two
Nueve	Nine
Ocho	Eight
Quince	Fifteen
Seis	Six
Siete	Seven
Trece	Thirteen
Tres	Three
Veinte	Twenty

Océano
Ocean

Alga	Algae
Anguila	Eel
Arrecife	Reef
Atún	Tuna
Ballena	Whale
Barco	Boat
Camarón	Shrimp
Cangrejo	Crab
Coral	Coral
Delfín	Dolphin
Esponja	Sponge
Mareas	Tides
Medusa	Jellyfish
Ostra	Oyster
Pescado	Fish
Pulpo	Octopus
Sal	Salt
Tiburón	Shark
Tormenta	Storm
Tortuga	Turtle

Paisajes
Landscapes

Cascada	Waterfall
Cueva	Cave
Desierto	Desert
Estuario	Estuary
Géiser	Geyser
Glaciar	Glacier
Iceberg	Iceberg
Isla	Island
Lago	Lake
Laguna	Lagoon
Mar	Sea
Montaña	Mountain
Oasis	Oasis
Pantano	Swamp
Península	Peninsula
Playa	Beach
Río	River
Tundra	Tundra
Valle	Valley
Volcán	Volcano

Países #2
Countries #2

Albania	Albania
Australia	Australia
Austria	Austria
Dinamarca	Denmark
Etiopía	Ethiopia
Francia	France
Grecia	Greece
Indonesia	Indonesia
Irlanda	Ireland
Jamaica	Jamaica
Japón	Japan
Laos	Laos
México	Mexico
Pakistán	Pakistan
Portugal	Portugal
Rusia	Russia
Siria	Syria
Sudán	Sudan
Ucrania	Ukraine
Uganda	Uganda

Pájaros
Birds

Avestruz	Ostrich
Águila	Eagle
Cigüeña	Stork
Cisne	Swan
Cuco	Cuckoo
Cuervo	Crow
Flamenco	Flamingo
Ganso	Goose
Garza	Heron
Gaviota	Gull
Gorrión	Sparrow
Halcón	Hawk
Huevo	Egg
Loro	Parrot
Paloma	Pigeon
Pato	Duck
Pelícano	Pelican
Pingüino	Penguin
Pollo	Chicken
Tucán	Toucan

Pesca
Fishing

Agua	Water
Aletas	Fins
Barco	Boat
Branquias	Gills
Cable	Wire
Cebo	Bait
Cesta	Basket
Cocinar	Cook
Equipo	Equipment
Exageración	Exaggeration
Gancho	Hook
Lago	Lake
Mandíbula	Jaw
Océano	Ocean
Paciencia	Patience
Peso	Weight
Playa	Beach
Río	River
Temporada	Season

Piratas
Pirates

Ancla	Anchor
Aventura	Adventure
Bandera	Flag
Brújula	Compass
Capitán	Captain
Cicatriz	Scar
Cueva	Cave
Espada	Sword
Isla	Island
Leyenda	Legend
Loro	Parrot
Malo	Bad
Mapa	Map
Monedas	Coins
Oro	Gold
Peligro	Danger
Playa	Beach
Ron	Rum
Tesoro	Treasure
Tripulación	Crew

Plantas
Plants

Arbusto	Bush
Árbol	Tree
Bambú	Bamboo
Baya	Berry
Bosque	Forest
Botánica	Botany
Cactus	Cactus
Fertilizante	Fertilizer
Flor	Flower
Flora	Flora
Follaje	Foliage
Frijol	Bean
Hiedra	Ivy
Hierba	Grass
Hoja	Leaf
Jardín	Garden
Musgo	Moss
Pétalo	Petal
Raíz	Root
Vegetación	Vegetation

Profesiones #1
Professions #1

Abogado	Attorney
Astrónomo	Astronomer
Atleta	Athlete
Bailarín	Dancer
Banquero	Banker
Bombero	Firefighter
Cartógrafo	Cartographer
Cazador	Hunter
Doctor	Doctor
Editor	Editor
Embajador	Ambassador
Enfermera	Nurse
Entrenador	Coach
Fontanero	Plumber
Geólogo	Geologist
Joyero	Jeweler
Músico	Musician
Pianista	Pianist
Psicólogo	Psychologist
Veterinario	Veterinarian

Profesiones #2
Professions #2

Astronauta	Astronaut
Bibliotecario	Librarian
Biólogo	Biologist
Cirujano	Surgeon
Dentista	Dentist
Detective	Detective
Filósofo	Philosopher
Fotógrafo	Photographer
Ilustrador	Illustrator
Ingeniero	Engineer
Inventor	Inventor
Investigador	Researcher
Jardinero	Gardener
Lingüista	Linguist
Médico	Physician
Periodista	Journalist
Piloto	Pilot
Pintor	Painter
Profesor	Teacher
Zoólogo	Zoologist

Rellenar
To Fill

Bandeja	Tray
Bañera	Tub
Barril	Barrel
Bolsa	Bag
Bolsillo	Pocket
Botella	Bottle
Caja	Box
Cajón	Drawer
Carpeta	Folder
Cartón	Carton
Cesta	Basket
Cubo	Bucket
Cuenca	Basin
Jarrón	Vase
Maleta	Suitcase
Paquete	Packet
Sobre	Envelope
Tarro	Jar
Tubo	Tube

Restaurante #1
Restaurant #1

Alergia	Allergy
Café	Coffee
Cajero	Cashier
Camarera	Waitress
Carne	Meat
Cocina	Kitchen
Comer	To Eat
Comida	Food
Cuchillo	Knife
Ingredientes	Ingredients
Menú	Menu
Pan	Bread
Picante	Spicy
Plato	Plate
Pollo	Chicken
Postre	Dessert
Reserva	Reservation
Salsa	Sauce
Servilleta	Napkin
Tazón	Bowl

Restaurante #2
Restaurant #2

Agua	Water
Almuerzo	Lunch
Aperitivo	Appetizer
Bebida	Beverage
Camarero	Waiter
Cena	Dinner
Cuchara	Spoon
Delicioso	Delicious
Ensalada	Salad
Especias	Spices
Fruta	Fruit
Hielo	Ice
Huevos	Eggs
Pastel	Cake
Pescado	Fish
Sal	Salt
Silla	Chair
Sopa	Soup
Tenedor	Fork
Verduras	Vegetables

Ropa
Clothes

Abrigo	Coat
Blusa	Blouse
Bufanda	Scarf
Camisa	Shirt
Chaqueta	Jacket
Cinturón	Belt
Collar	Necklace
Delantal	Apron
Falda	Skirt
Guantes	Gloves
Joyas	Jewelry
Moda	Fashion
Pantalones	Pants
Pijama	Pajamas
Pulsera	Bracelet
Sandalias	Sandals
Sombrero	Hat
Suéter	Sweater
Vestido	Dress
Zapato	Shoe

Selva Tropical
Rainforest

Anfibios	Amphibians
Botánico	Botanical
Clima	Climate
Comunidad	Community
Diversidad	Diversity
Especie	Species
Indígena	Indigenous
Insectos	Insects
Mamíferos	Mammals
Musgo	Moss
Naturaleza	Nature
Nubes	Clouds
Pájaros	Birds
Preservación	Preservation
Refugio	Refuge
Respeto	Respect
Restauración	Restoration
Selva	Jungle
Supervivencia	Survival
Valioso	Valuable

Senderismo
Hiking

Acantilado	Cliff
Agua	Water
Animales	Animals
Botas	Boots
Camping	Camping
Cansado	Tired
Clima	Climate
Cumbre	Summit
Guías	Guides
Mapa	Map
Montaña	Mountain
Mosquitos	Mosquitoes
Naturaleza	Nature
Orientación	Orientation
Parques	Parks
Pesado	Heavy
Piedras	Stones
Preparación	Preparation
Salvaje	Wild
Sol	Sun

Suministros de Arte
Art Supplies

Aceite	Oil
Acrílico	Acrylic
Acuarelas	Watercolors
Agua	Water
Arcilla	Clay
Borrador	Eraser
Caballete	Easel
Cámara	Camera
Cepillos	Brushes
Colores	Colors
Creatividad	Creativity
Ideas	Ideas
Lápices	Pencils
Mesa	Table
Papel	Paper
Pasteles	Pastels
Pegamento	Glue
Pinturas	Paints
Silla	Chair
Tinta	Ink

Surf
Surfing

Arrecife	Reef
Atleta	Athlete
Campeón	Champion
Clima	Weather
Diversión	Fun
Espuma	Foam
Estilo	Style
Estómago	Stomach
Extremo	Extreme
Fuerza	Strength
Multitudes	Crowds
Nadar	To Swim
Océano	Ocean
Ola	Wave
Playa	Beach
Popular	Popular
Principiante	Beginner
Remo	Paddle
Rociar	Spray
Velocidad	Speed

Tecnología
Technology

Archivo	File
Blog	Blog
Bytes	Bytes
Cámara	Camera
Cursor	Cursor
Datos	Data
Digital	Digital
Estadísticas	Statistics
Fuente	Font
Internet	Internet
Investigación	Research
Mensaje	Message
Navegador	Browser
Ordenador	Computer
Pantalla	Screen
Seguridad	Security
Software	Software
Virtual	Virtual
Virus	Virus

Tiempo
Time

Ahora	Now
Antes	Before
Anual	Annual
Año	Year
Ayer	Yesterday
Calendario	Calendar
Década	Decade
Día	Day
Futuro	Future
Hora	Hour
Hoy	Today
Mañana	Morning
Mediodía	Noon
Mes	Month
Minuto	Minute
Momento	Moment
Noche	Night
Reloj	Clock
Semana	Week
Siglo	Century

Tipos de Cabello
Hair Types

Blanco	White
Brillante	Shiny
Calvo	Bald
Corto	Short
Delgada	Thin
Gris	Gray
Grueso	Thick
Largo	Long
Marrón	Brown
Negro	Black
Ondulado	Wavy
Plata	Silver
Rizado	Curly
Rizos	Curls
Rubio	Blond
Saludable	Healthy
Seco	Dry
Suave	Soft
Trenzado	Braided
Trenzas	Braids

Vacaciones #2
Vacation #2

Aeropuerto	Airport
Carpa	Tent
Destino	Destination
Extranjero	Foreigner
Fotos	Photos
Hotel	Hotel
Isla	Island
Mapa	Map
Mar	Sea
Montañas	Mountains
Ocio	Leisure
Pasaporte	Passport
Playa	Beach
Reservas	Reservations
Restaurante	Restaurant
Taxi	Taxi
Tren	Train
Vacaciones	Holiday
Viaje	Journey
Visa	Visa

Vehículos
Vehicles

Ambulancia	Ambulance
Autobús	Bus
Avión	Airplane
Balsa	Raft
Barco	Boat
Bicicleta	Bicycle
Camión	Truck
Caravana	Caravan
Coche	Car
Cohete	Rocket
Ferry	Ferry
Helicóptero	Helicopter
Lanzadera	Shuttle
Metro	Subway
Motor	Motor
Neumáticos	Tires
Submarino	Submarine
Taxi	Taxi
Tractor	Tractor
Tren	Train

Verano
Summer

Alegría	Joy
Amigos	Friends
Buceo	Diving
Comida	Food
Estrellas	Stars
Familia	Family
Hogar	Home
Jardín	Garden
Juegos	Games
Libros	Books
Mar	Sea
Música	Music
Nadar	To Swim
Ocio	Leisure
Playa	Beach
Recuerdos	Memories
Relajación	Relaxation
Sandalias	Sandals
Vacaciones	Vacation
Viaje	Travel

Verduras
Vegetables

Ajo	Garlic
Alcachofa	Artichoke
Apio	Celery
Berenjena	Eggplant
Brócoli	Broccoli
Calabaza	Pumpkin
Cebolla	Onion
Ensalada	Salad
Espinacas	Spinach
Guisante	Pea
Jengibre	Ginger
Nabo	Turnip
Oliva	Olive
Patata	Potato
Pepino	Cucumber
Perejil	Parsley
Rábano	Radish
Seta	Mushroom
Tomate	Tomato
Zanahoria	Carrot

Virtudes #1
Virtues #1

Apasionado	Passionate
Artístico	Artistic
Bien	Good
Curioso	Curious
Decisivo	Decisive
Eficiente	Efficient
Encantador	Charming
Fiable	Reliable
Generoso	Generous
Gracioso	Funny
Imaginativo	Imaginative
Independiente	Independent
Inteligente	Intelligent
Limpio	Clean
Modesto	Modest
Paciente	Patient
Práctico	Practical
Sabio	Wise
Útil	Helpful

Enhorabuena

Lo has conseguido!

Esperamos que hayas disfrutado de este libro tanto como nosotros al diseñarlo. Nos esforzamos por crear libros de la máxima calidad posible.
Esta edición está diseñada para proporcionar un aprendizaje inteligente, de calidad y divertido!

¿Te ha gustado este libro?

Una Petición Sencilla

Estos libros existen gracias a las reseñas que se publican.
¿Podrías ayudarnos dejando una reseña ahora?
Aquí tienes un breve enlace a la página de reseñas

BestBooksActivity.com/Opiniones50

¡DESAFÍO FINAL!

Reto n°1

¿Estás listo para tu juego gratis? Los utilizamos siempre, pero no son tan fáciles de encontrar. ¡Aquí están los **Sinónimos!**

Escribe 5 palabras que hayas encontrado en los rompecabezas (#21, #36, #76) y trata de encontrar 2 sinónimos para cada palabra.

Escriba 5 palabras del *Puzzle 21*

Palabras	Sinónimo 1	Sinónimo 2

Escriba 5 palabras del *Puzzle 36*

Palabras	Sinónimo 1	Sinónimo 2

Escriba 5 palabras del *Puzzle 76*

Palabras	Sinónimo 1	Sinónimo 2

Reto n°2

Ahora que te has calentado, escribe 5 palabras que hayas encontrado en los Puzzles 9, 17 y 25 e intenta encontrar 2 antónimos para cada palabra. ¿Cuántos puedes encontrar en 20 minutos?

Escriba 5 palabras del **Puzzle 9**

Palabras	Antónimo 1	Antónimo 2

Escriba 5 palabras del **Puzzle 17**

Palabras	Antónimo 1	Antónimo 2

Escriba 5 palabras del **Puzzle 25**

Palabras	Antónimo 1	Antónimo 2

Reto n°3

¡Genial! Este desafío final no es nada para ti.

¿Preparado para el reto final? Elige 10 palabras que hayas descubierto en los diferentes rompecabezas y escríbelas a continuación.

1.	6.
2.	7.
3.	8.
4.	9.
5.	10.

Ahora escribe un texto pensando en una persona, un animal o un lugar que te guste.

Puedes usar la última página de este libro como borrador.

Tu Composición:

CUADERNO DE NOTAS :

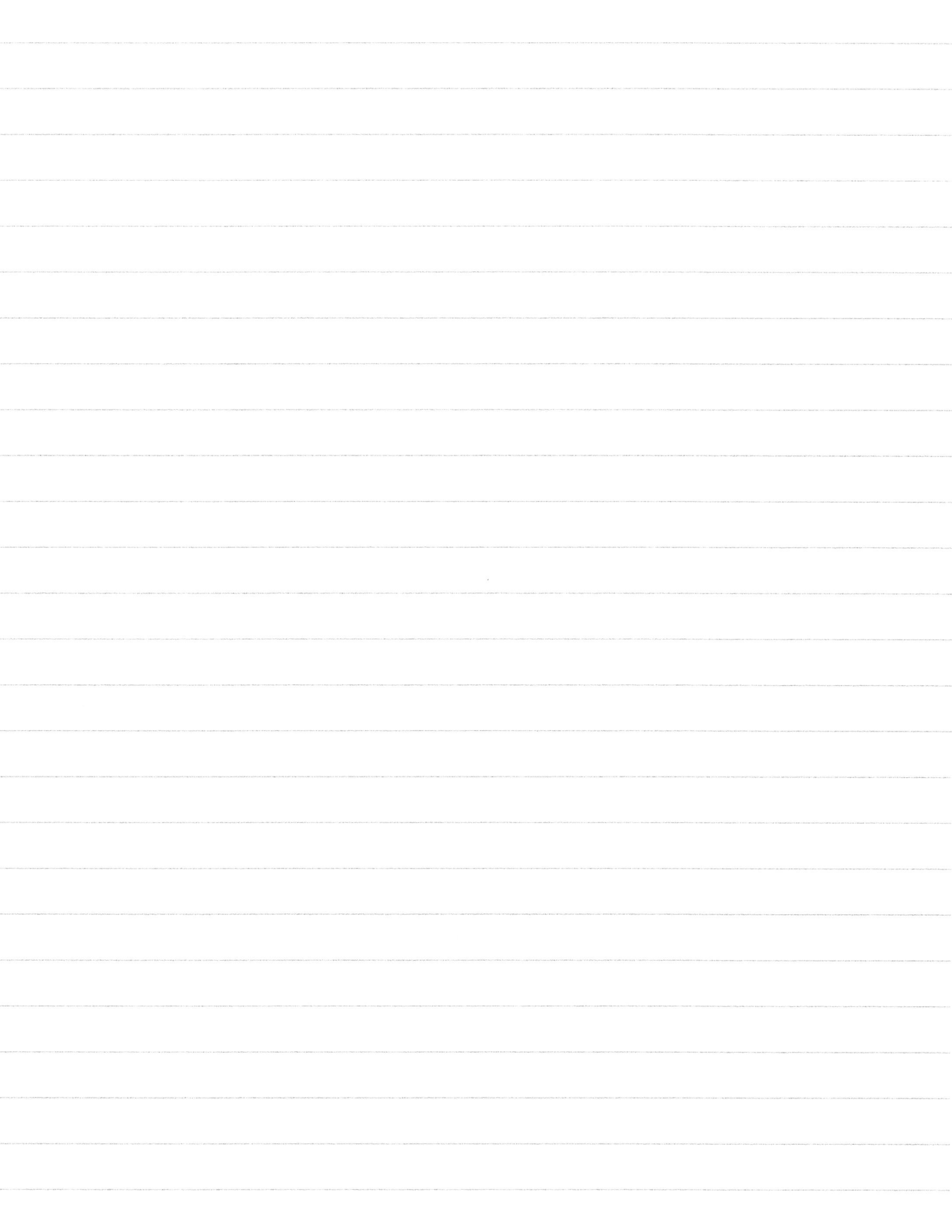

HASTA PRONTO !

Todo el Equipo

DESCUBRA JUEGOS GRATIS

GO

↓

BESTACTIVITYBOOKS.COM/FREEGAMES